BEGINNING

PYTHON

PROGRAMMING

A COMPLETE READYMADE SOLUTION
FOR YOUR PYTHON LEARNING COURSE AT ONE PLACE
STEP - BY - STEP

SHIKHA KESARWANI

CONTENTS

PYTHON PROGRAMMING DETAILED

= DIFFERENT DATA TYPE TO

= DIFFERENT DATA TYPE

= INT ← CONVERTING BOOLEAN

= INTEGER ← CONVERTING TRUE

= INTEGER ← CONVERTING FALSE

= **int() function** ← BOOLEAN EXPRESSION

= INTEGER ← CONVERTING TRUE

= INTEGER ← CONVERTING FALSE

= **str() function** ← BOOLEAN EXPRESSION

= STRING ← CONVERTING TRUE

= STRING ← CONVERTING FALSE

= **format() , f-string function** ← BOOLEAN EXPRESSION

= STRING ← CONVERTING TRUE

= STRING ← CONVERTING FALSE

= **bool() function** ← CONVERTING NUMBER

= BOOLEAN ← CONVERTING ZERO

= BOOLEAN ← CONVERTING NON - ZERO

= **bool() function** ← FLOATING - POINT NUMBER

= BOOLEAN ← FLOATING - POINT NUMBER

= ADDITION (+)

= SUBTRACTION (-)

= MULTIPLICATION (*)

= DIVISION (/)

= FLOOR DIVISION (//)

= MODULUS (%)

= **OPERATORS ← BITWISE**

= BITWISE AND (&)

= BITWISE OR (|)

= BITWISE XOR (^)

= BITWISE NOT (~)

= LEFT SHIFT (<<)

= RIGHT SHIFT (>>)

= **OPERATORS ← COMPARISON**

= EQUAL TO (==)

= NOT EQUAL TO (!=)

= GREATER THAN (>)

= LESS THAN (<)

= GREATER THAN OR EQUAL TO (>=)

= LESS THAN OR EQUAL TO (<=)

INTRODUCTION

If you are a beginner or you are software professional easy to learn.

The syntax is simple, clean and organized code. Easy to understand and learn.

Python is most popular programming language in current time.

Here, you will get all required basic concepts and required resource in few days you will be comfortable with Python programming.

Learn Python variables,Boolean,number data types,true false,string data types,converting data types,if statements,while loop,for loop,function.

In Data structures introduction list,tuple,dictionary,set,adding,inserting,accessing,modifying,removing elements.

Sorting,reversing,slicing and shuffling elements in list,tuple,dictionary,set.

Modules,class,inheritance,abstract class,operator overloading,files,text file,exception,testing.

CHAPTER 1

PYTHON ← INTRODUCTION

- ≡ Python's popularity stems from its simplicity, versatility, and robustness.

Here are some of its main features.

READABLE AND SIMPLE SYNTAX:

- ≡ Python's syntax is designed to be easy to read and write, making it accessible to beginners and experienced programmers alike.
- ≡ It emphasizes readability, reducing the cost of program maintenance and development.

EXTENSIVE STANDARD LIBRARY:

- ≡ Python comes with a large standard library that provides modules and packages for various tasks such as string manipulation, file I/O, networking, and more.
- ≡ This extensive library reduces the need for additional third-party modules and simplifies development.

DYNAMIN TYPING , DYNAMIC BINDING:

- ≡ Python is dynamically typed, meaning you don't need to declare the type of variables.

- ≡ Python features dynamic binding, which means that variable names are bound to objects at runtime, providing more flexibility in code structure.

CROSS - PLATEFORM COMPATIBILITY:

- ≡ Python is available for all major operating systems (Windows, macOS, Linux) and is portable across platforms.
- ≡ This allows developers to write code once and run it anywhere, making it highly versatile.

OPEN SOURCE:

- ≡ Python is open source, meaning its source code is freely available and can be modified and redistributed by anyone.

These features collectively contribute to Python's popularity and widespread adoption in various domains such as web development, data science, machine learning, artificial intelligence, scientific computing, automation, and more.

PYTHON ← INSTALLATION OF COMPILER

- Python is an interpreted language.
- So it doesn't require compilation in the traditional sense.
- You require Python interpreter on your system to run Python code.

DOWNLOAD INSTALLER:

STEP 1:

VISIT PYTHON WEBSITE:

- Go to the official Python website at https://www.python.org/.

STEP 2:

DOWNLOAD PYTHON:

- On the homepage, you'll see a prominent button for downloading Python.
- Click on it to navigate to the download page.

STEP 3:

CHOOSE INSTALLER:

- You'll be presented with different versions of Python.

- ✓ Typically, you'll want to download the latest stable version for your operating system (Windows, macOS, or Linux).
- ✓ Python distributions are available for both 32-bit and 64-bit systems.

STEP 4:

DOWNLOAD INSTALLER:

≡ Click on the download link for the installer that matches your operating system and architecture.

INSTALLE INSTALLER:

STEP 1:

RUN INSTALLER:

≡ Once the installer is downloaded, run it by double-clicking on the downloaded file.

STEP 2:

FOLLOW INSTALLATION WIZARD:

≡ The installation wizard will guide you through the installation process.
≡ You can choose the installation directory, customize the installation options if needed, and install additional features like pip (Python's package manager) and adding Python to the system PATH (recommended).

STEP 3:

COMPLETE INSTALLATION:

≡ Once you've configured the installation options, proceed with the installation.
≡ The installer will copy the necessary files to your system and set up Python.

STEP 4:

VERIFY INSTALLATION:

≡ After the installation is complete, you can verify that Python is installed correctly by opening a command prompt.

WINDOWS:

```
python –version
```

MACOS / LINUX:

```
python3 –version
```

This should display the installed Python version.

PYTHON : FIRST PROGRAMME

PYTHON ← HELLO WORLD

≡ Writing "Hello, World!" to the console in Python is straightforward.

Here's the code.

```python
print("Hello, World!")
```

You can write this code in a text editor.

OR

An integrated development environment (IDE) such as Visual Studio Code, PyCharm, or IDLE.

Save the file with a .py extension, such as hello_world.py.

TO RUN PYTHON CODE , SEE OUTPUT IN CONSOLE

STEP 1:

OPEN COMMAND PROMPT:

≡ Open a command prompt (**WINDOWS**)   or
≡ terminal (**MACOS / LINUX**).

STEP 2:

NAVIGATE DIRECTORY:

≡ Navigate to the directory where your Python file (hello_world.py) is saved using the cd command.

STEP 3:

EXECUTING PYTHON SCRIPT:

- ≡ Once you're in the correct directory.
- ≡ Type python hello_world.py and press Enter (or python3 hello_world.py on some systems).

This will execute the Python script, and you should see.

```
"Hello, World!"
```

Printed to the console.

PYTHON ← COMMENTS

- ≡ In Python, you can write comments to document your code or provide explanations.
- ≡ Comments are ignored by the Python interpreter and are meant for human readers.

EXAMPLE

```python
# This is a single-line comment
print("Hello, World!")


# This is a comment ,  multiple lines comment
# This is another comment
print("Hello, World!")


"""
This is a multi-line comment.
You can write multiple lines of text within triple quotes.
This is often used as a docstring for documenting functions or modules.
"""
print("Hello, World!")
```

VARIABLES : INTRODUCTION

- ≡ In Python, variables are used to store data values.
- ≡ A variable is a name that refers to a value stored in memory.

- ≡ Unlike some other programming languages, Python is dynamically typed, meaning you don't need to declare the type of a variable before assigning a value to it.

VARIABLE ← ASSIGNMENT

You can assign a value to a variable using the = operator.

```
x = 10
name = "Alice"
```

VARIABLE ← NAMING RULES

- ≡ Variable names must start with a letter (a-z, A-Z) or an underscore _.
- ≡ Variable names can contain letters, digits (0-9), and underscores _.
- ≡ Variable names are case-sensitive (name and Name are different variables).
- ≡ Python keywords (e.g., if, for, while, def, etc.) cannot be used as variable names.

DATA TYPE:

Python variables can hold values of different data types, including.

- ≡ Integer (int): Whole numbers, e.g., 10, -5, 1000.
- ≡ Float (float): Floating-point numbers, e.g., 3.14, 2.718.
- ≡ String (str): Sequence of characters, e.g., "Hello", 'Python'.
- ≡ Boolean (bool): Represents True or False.
- ≡ List (list), Tuple (tuple), Dictionary (dict), Set (set), etc.

```
age = 25            # integer
pi = 3.14           # float
name = "Alice"      # string
is_student = True   # Boolean
```

VARIABLE ← REASSIGNMENT

- ≡ You can change the value of a variable by assigning a new value to it.

```
x = 5
x = x + 1  # x now holds the value 6
```

VARIABLE ← SCOPE

- ≡ Variables have a scope, which defines where they can be accessed from.
- ≡ Variables declared inside a function have local scope, meaning they are only accessible within that function.
- ≡ Variables declared outside of any function have global scope and can be accessed from anywhere in the code.

```
x = 10       # global variable

def my_function():
    y = 20    # local variable
    print(x)  # x can be accessed here
    print(y)  # y can be accessed here


my_function()
print(x)     # x can be accessed here
print(y)     # Error: y is not defined
```

Variables are fundamental to programming in Python, as they allow you to store and manipulate data within your programs.

CHAPTER 2

BOOLEAN , NUMBER

UNDERSTANDING BOOLEAN , NUMBER DATA TYPES

BOOLEAN ← INTRODUCTION

- ≡ **Boolean** values are a data type in Python that represent truth values.
- ≡ They can only have one of two values: True or False.
- ≡ **Boolean** values are commonly used in conditional statements, loops, and logical operations to control the flow of the program or to represent the result of a comparison.

BOOLEAN ← USING BOOLEAN

BOOLEAN VARIABLES:

- ≡ You can assign Boolean values to variables like any other data type.

```
is_student = True
has_passed_exam = False
```

CONDITIONAL STATEMENTS:

≡ Boolean values are often used in conditional statements (if, elif, else) to execute different blocks of code based on whether a condition is True or False.

```
if is_student:
    print("The person is a student.")
else:
    print("The person is not a student.")
```

LOGICAL OPERATORS:

≡ Boolean values can be combined using logical operators (and, or, not) to create compound conditions.

```
age = 20
is_adult = age >= 18
is_teenager = age >= 13 and age <= 19
```

LOOPS:

≡ Boolean values are often used as loop conditions to control the execution of the loop.

```
while is_student:
    print("Still studying...")

    # Some condition to update is_student, otherwise, it may
        result in an infinite loop
```

```
  is_student = False
```

FUNCTION RETURNS:

≡ Functions can return Boolean values to indicate the success or failure of an operation or to indicate a condition.

```python
def is_even(number):
    return number % 2 == 0


print(is_even(4))  # True
print(is_even(5))  # False
```

BUILT - IN FUNCTIONS:

≡ Python provides built-in functions like bool() to convert other data types to Boolean values.

```python
print(bool(0))    # False
print(bool(1))    # True
print(bool([]))    # False (empty list)
print(bool([1]))  # True (non-empty list)
```

Boolean values play a crucial role in programming as they enable you to make decisions, control program flow, and perform logical operations.

TRUE FALSE : EXPLORING AT ONCE

- ≡ In Python, True and False are the two boolean values that represent the truth values.
- ≡ They are used to control the flow of the program, make decisions, and perform logical operations.

Here are some important notes on True and False and how to use them in Python:

TRUE AND FALSE VALUES:

- ✓ True and False are reserved keywords in Python.
- ✓ True represents the truth value true, while False represents the truth value false.
- ✓ These are the only two boolean values in Python.

BOOLEAN OPERATIONS:

- ✓ Boolean values are commonly used in logical operations such as AND (and), OR (or), and NOT (not).
- ✓ The and operator returns True if both operands are true, otherwise it returns False.
- ✓ The or operator returns True if at least one of the operands is true, otherwise it returns False.
- ✓ The not operator returns the opposite boolean value of its operand.

COMPARISON OPERATORS:

- ✓ Comparison operators (==, !=, <, <=, >, >=) return boolean values (True or False) based on the comparison result.

✓ For example, $x == y$ returns True if x is equal to y, otherwise it returns False.

CONTROL STRUCTURES:

✓ Boolean values are extensively used in control structures such as if, elif, else statements and loops (while, for).
✓ These structures allow you to execute different blocks of code based on conditions evaluated to True or False.

TRUTHINESS AND FALSINESS:

✓ In addition to True and False, other values in Python can be evaluated as either true or false in a boolean context.
✓ Values such as empty sequences (lists, tuples, strings, etc.), 0, and None are evaluated as False. Any non-zero number or non-empty sequence is evaluated as True.

RETURN VALUES:

✓ Functions can return boolean values to indicate the success or failure of an operation or to represent a condition.
✓ For example, a function that checks if a number is even might return True or False based on the result of the check.

NUMBER DATA TYPES : INTRODUCTION

Python supports several numerical data types, each with its own characteristics and use cases. Here are the main numerical data types that Python can handle:

INTEGER (int):

- Integers represent whole numbers without any decimal point.
- Example: 5, -10, 1000.

FLOATING - POINT (float):

- Floating-point numbers represent real numbers with a decimal point.
- Example: 3.14, 2.718, -0.5.

DECIMAL (decimal.Decimal):

- Decimal numbers represent fixed-point decimal numbers with arbitrary precision.
- They are useful for financial and other applications requiring exact decimal representations.
- Example: Decimal('3.14'), Decimal('10.5').

FRACTION (fractions.Fraction):

- Fraction numbers represent rational numbers as fractions of integers.
- They are useful for exact representation of fractions.
- Example: Fraction(3, 4), Fraction(5, 2).

BOOLEAN (bool):

- ≡ Boolean values represent truth values, which can be either True or False.
- ≡ They are commonly used for logical operations and control flow.
- ≡ Example: True, False.

INTEGER ← INTRODUCTION

- ≡ Creating integer numbers and performing simple calculations in Python is straightforward.

You can define integer variables and use mathematical operators to perform calculations.

EXAMPLE

```python
# Create integer variables
x = 5
y = 3


# Perform arithmetic operations
sum_result = x + y
difference_result = x - y
product_result = x * y
quotient_result = x / y        # Division returns a float in
                                 Python 3.x
```

```
floor_division_result = x // y  # Floor division returns an
                                       integer
remainder_result = x % y       # Modulus operator returns the
                                       remainder
# Print the results
print("Sum:", sum_result)
print("Difference:", difference_result)
print("Product:", product_result)
print("Quotient:", quotient_result)
print("Floor Division:", floor_division_result)
print("Remainder:", remainder_result)
```

OUTPUT

```
Sum: 8
Difference: 2
Product: 15
Quotient: 1.6666666666666667
Floor Division: 1
Remainder: 2
```

EXPLANATION

- ≡ We create two integer variables x and y.
- ≡ We perform simple arithmetic operations using the +, -, *, /, //, and % operators.
- ≡ We print the results of the calculations.

✓ You can perform various arithmetic operations on integer numbers in Python, including addition, subtraction, multiplication, division, floor division, and modulus.

✓ Depending on the operands and operators used, Python will return the appropriate result, which can be an integer or a floating-point number.

FLOAT ← INTRODUCTION

≡ Creating floating-point numbers and performing simple calculations in Python is similar to working with integer numbers.

We will learn creating floating-point variables and performing arithmetic operations:

EXAMPLE

```python
# Create floating-point variables
x = 3.5
y = 2.0

# Perform arithmetic operations
sum_result = x + y
difference_result = x - y
product_result = x * y
quotient_result = x / y
```

```
# Print the results
print("Sum:", sum_result)
print("Difference:", difference_result)
print("Product:", product_result)
print("Quotient:", quotient_result)
```

OUTPUT

```
Sum: 5.5
Difference: 1.5
Product: 7.0
Quotient: 1.75
```

EXPLANATION

- ≡ You can use the same arithmetic operators (+, -, *, /, //, %) as with integer numbers to perform calculations with floating-point numbers.
- ≡ However, it's important to note that when performing division (/), Python will always return a floating-point result, even if the operands are integers.

- ≡ We create two floating-point variables x and y.
- ≡ We perform simple arithmetic operations using the +, -, *, and / operators.
- ≡ We print the results of the calculations.

CHAPTER 3

STRING IN PYTHON

STRING ← INTRODUCTION

Creating a variable ← And assigning a string value to it

EXAMPLE

```python
# Create a variable named 'my_string' and assign a string value to it
my_string = "Hello, World!"
# Print the value of the variable
print(my_string)
```

OUTPUT

```
Hello, World!
```

EXPLANATION

- ≡ We create a variable named my_string.
- ≡ We use the assignment operator = to assign the string "Hello, World!" to the variable my_string.
- ≡ We then print the value of my_string using the print() function.
- ✓ You can assign any string value to a variable in Python.
- ✓ And the variable will hold that value until it is changed or deleted.

STRING ← VARIABLE

- ≡ In Python, you can use variables inside strings using string formatting techniques.
- ≡ There are several ways to achieve this, including using the % operator, the str.format() method, and f-strings (formatted string literals).

Here's how you can use variables inside strings using each method:

Here you will learn same idea in three different ways.

USING % OPERATOR:

You can use the % operator to insert variables into strings.

This method is older and less recommended compared to newer methods like f-strings and str.format().

EXAMPLE

```
name = "Alice"
age = 30
greeting = "Hello, %s! You are %d years old." % (name, age)
print(greeting)
```

OUTPUT

```
Hello, Alice! You are 30 years old.
```

USING str.format() METHOD:

The str.format() method allows you to format strings with placeholders {} that are replaced with variable values.

EXAMPLE

```
name = "Alice"
age = 30
greeting = "Hello, {}! You are {} years old.".format(name,
age)
print(greeting)
```

OUTPUT

```
Hello, Alice! You are 30 years old.
```

USING f-strings (FORMATTED STRING LITERALS):

F-strings provide a more concise and readable way to insert variables into strings.

You can directly include variables and expressions within curly braces {} inside the string.

EXAMPLE

```
name = "Alice"
age = 30
greeting = f"Hello, {name}! You are {age} years old."
print(greeting)
```

OUTPUT

```
Hello, Alice! You are 30 years old.
```

String ← Escape

- ≡ Escape sequences in Python strings are special characters that are preceded by a backslash \.
- ≡ These sequences allow you to include characters in strings that are difficult or impossible to type directly in source code.

Here are some commonly used escape sequences in Python.

\n: Newline Character:

Newline character. It inserts a newline into the string.

Example

```
print("Line 1\nLine 2")
```

Output

```
Line 1
Line 2
```

\t: Tab Character:

Tab character. It inserts a horizontal tab into the string.

Example

```
print("Column 1\tColumn 2")
```

Output

```
Column 1    Column 2
```

\r: Carriage Return Character:

Carriage return character. It moves the cursor to the beginning of the line.

EXAMPLE

```
print("Hello\rWorld")
```

OUTPUT

```
World
```

\\: BACKSLASH CHARACTER:

Backslash character. It inserts a literal backslash into the string.

EXAMPLE

```
print("This is a backslash: \\")
```

OUTPUT

```
This is a backslash: \
```

String ← Whitespace

≡ In Python, you can strip whitespace (spaces, tabs, newlines) from the beginning and end of a string using the strip() method.

Here's how you can use it:

EXAMPLE

```python
# Original string with whitespace
original_string = "   Hello, World!   "

# Strip whitespace from the beginning and end of the string
stripped_string = original_string.strip()

# Print the stripped string
print(stripped_string)
```

OUTPUT

```
Hello, World!
```

The strip() method removes leading and trailing whitespace from the string.

If you only want to remove leading whitespace (at the beginning) or trailing whitespace (at the end), you can use the lstrip() or rstrip() methods, respectively.

EXAMPLE

```python
# Original string with whitespace
```

```
original_string = "   Hello, World!   "

# Strip leading whitespace from the string
left_stripped_string = original_string.lstrip()

# Strip trailing whitespace from the string
right_stripped_string = original_string.rstrip()

# Print the stripped strings
print(left_stripped_string)
print(right_stripped_string)
```

OUTPUT

```
Hello, World!
   Hello, World!
```

- ≡ In addition to strip(), lstrip(), and rstrip(), you can also specify the characters you want to strip as an argument to these methods.
- ≡ For example, strip("x") would strip all occurrences of the character 'x' from the beginning and end of the string.
- ≡ Similarly, lstrip("x") and rstrip("x") would only strip occurrences of 'x' from the left or right side of the string, respectively.
- ≡ If no argument is provided, the methods will strip all whitespace characters by default.

String ← Prefixes

≡ To remove prefixes from a Python string, you can use various methods depending on your specific requirements.

Here are some common approaches.

Using str.startswith() With Slicing:

≡ If you know the prefix you want to remove and you want to remove it only if it appears at the beginning of the string, you can use the str.startswith() method along with slicing.

Example

```python
# Original string with prefix
original_string = "prefix_hello_world"

# Prefix to remove
prefix = "prefix_"

# Check if the string starts with the prefix
if original_string.startswith(prefix):
    # Remove the prefix using slicing
    modified_string = original_string[len(prefix):]
else:
    modified_string = original_string
```

```
print(modified_string)
```

OUTPUT

```
hello_world
```

USING str.removeprefix():

≡ str.removeprefix() method, which specifically removes a prefix from the string if it is present.

This method is more concise and readable.

EXAMPLE

```
# Original string with prefix
original_string = "prefix_hello_world"
# Prefix to remove
prefix = "prefix_"
# Remove the prefix using str.removeprefix()
modified_string = original_string.removeprefix(prefix)
print(modified_string)
```

OUTPUT

```
hello_world
```

CHAPTER 4

CONVERTING

DIFFERENT DATA TYPE TO DIFFERENT DATA TYPE

INT ← CONVERTING BOOLEAN

- ≡ In Python, you can convert a Boolean value to an integer using the int() function.
- ≡ When you convert a Boolean value to an integer, True is represented as 1 and False is represented as 0.

Here's how you can do it.

INTEGER ← CONVERTING TRUE

EXAMPLE

```
boolean_value = True
integer_value = int(boolean_value)
print(integer_value)
```

OUTPUT

```
1
```

INTEGER ← CONVERTING FALSE

EXAMPLE

```python
# Convert False to integer
boolean_value = False


integer_value = int(boolean_value)
print(integer_value)
```

OUTPUT

```
0
```

int() function ← BOOLEAN EXPRESSION

INTEGER ← CONVERTING BOOLEAN EXPRESSION (TRUE)

EXAMPLE

Using int() function.

```
# Convert the result of a Boolean expression to integer
integer_value = int(10 > 5)  # Result of the expression is True
print(integer_value)
```

OUTPUT

```
1
```

INTEGER ← CONVERTING BOOLEAN EXPRESSION (FALSE)

EXAMPLE

Using int() function.

```
integer_value = int(10 < 5)  # Result of the expression is False
print(integer_value)
```

OUTPUT

```
0
```

- ✓ In Python, Boolean values are subclasses of integers, with True being equivalent to 1 and False being equivalent to 0.
- ✓ Therefore, when you use int() to convert a Boolean value to an integer, it simply returns the corresponding integer representation.

str() function ← CONVERTING BOOLEAN EXPRESSION

≡ In Python, you can convert a boolean value to a string using either the str() function or by using string formatting methods.

Here's how you can do it.

STRING ← CONVERTING BOOLEAN EXPRESSION (TRUE)

EXAMPLE

Using str() function.

```python
# Convert True to string , Using str() function.
boolean_value = True


string_value = str(boolean_value)
print(string_value)
```

OUTPUT

```
True
```

STRING ← CONVERTING BOOLEAN EXPRESSION (FALSE)

EXAMPLE

Using str() function.

```python
# Convert False to string
```

```
boolean_value = False


string_value = str(boolean_value)

print(string_value)
```

OUTPUT

```
False
```

STRING ← CONVERTING BOOLEAN EXPRESSION

(**U S I N G** string formatting format() , f-string function)

STRING ← CONVERTING BOOLEAN EXPRESSION (TRUE)

EXAMPLE

Using format() function.

```
# Convert True to string using formatting , format() function
boolean_value = True


string_value = "{}".format(boolean_value)
print(string_value)
```

OUTPUT

```
True
```

STRING ← CONVERTING BOOLEAN EXPRESSION (FALSE)

EXAMPLE

Using f-string function.

```
# Convert False to string using f-string
boolean_value = False


string_value = f"{boolean_value}"
print(string_value)
```

OUTPUT

```
False
```

- ✓ In both cases, the boolean value is converted to its string representation, either "True" or "False".
- ✓ This can be useful when you need to represent boolean values as strings for display or when working with string manipulation functions.

bool() function ← CONVERTING NUMBER

≡ In Python, numbers can be used in a boolean context, meaning they can be evaluated as either True or False depending on their value.

Here's how numbers are evaluated in a boolean context.

BOOLEAN ← CONVERTING ZERO

EXAMPLE

Using bool() function.

Any numeric value that is equal to zero (0) is evaluated as False.

```
# Convert Zero to boolean, Using bool() function.
zero_number = 0


boolean_value = bool(zero_number)
print(boolean_value)
```

OUTPUT

```
False
```

BOOLEAN ← CONVERTING NON - ZERO

EXAMPLE

Using bool() function.

Any numeric value that is not equal to zero (non-zero) is evaluated as True.

```python
# Convert Non-Zero to boolean, Using bool() function.
non_zero_number = 42


boolean_value = bool(non_zero_number)
print(boolean_value)
```

OUTPUT

```
True
```

bool() function ← FLOATING - POINT NUMBER

BOOLEAN ← CONVERTING FLOATING - POINT NUMBER

EXAMPLE

Using bool() function.

If the floating-point number is equal to zero, it's False, otherwise it's True.

```python
# Convert Floating-Point Numbers to boolean, Using bool()
   function.
floating_point_number = 0.0
boolean_value = bool(floating_point_number)
print(boolean_value)
```

OUTPUT

```
False
```

BOOLEAN ← CONVERTING FLOATING - POINT NUMBER

EXAMPLE

Using bool() function.

If the floating-point number is equal to zero, it's False, otherwise it's True.

```
# Convert Floating-Point Numbers to boolean, Using bool()
    function.
non_zero_float = 3.14


boolean_value = bool(non_zero_float)
print(boolean_value)
```

OUTPUT

```
True
```

(>, ==) operator ← CONVERTING NUMBER

BOOLEAN ← CONVERTING NUMBER

EXAMPLE

Using > operator.

Numbers are commonly used in comparisons, and the result of a comparison is a boolean value (True or False).

```python
# Convert Numbers to boolean, Using > operator
x = 5
y = 10
is_greater = x > y
print(is_greater)
```

OUTPUT

```
False
```

BOOLEAN ← CONVERTING NUMBER

EXAMPLE

Using == operator.

```python
# Convert Numbers to boolean, Using == operator
is_equal = x == 5
print(is_equal)
```

OUTPUT

```
True
```

CHAPTER 5

CONVERTING

STRING , FLOAT ← INTEGER

INTEGER , FLOAT ← STRING

str() , f-string , float() function ← CONVERTING

STRING , FLOAT ← CONVERTING INTEGER

STRING ← CONVERTING INTEGER

EXAMPLE

Using str() function.

```
# Convert an integer to a string , Using str() function
number = 123
string_number = str(number)

# Print the string representation
print(string_number)
```

OUTPUT

```
123
```

EXPLANATION

≡ In this example, the str() function is used to convert the integer 123 to a string representation "123".

≡ The resulting string can then be used in string operations, printed, or stored in a variable for further processing.

STRING ← CONVERTING INTEGER

EXAMPLE

Using f-string function.

```
# Using f-string to convert an integer to a string
number = 123
string_number = f"{number}"


# Print the string representation
print(string_number)
```

OUTPUT

```
123
```

FLOAT ← CONVERTING INTEGER

EXAMPLE

Using float() function.

```
# Convert an integer to a floating-point number , Using float()
function

integer_number = 123

float_number = float(integer_number)


# Print the floating-point number

print(float_number)
```

OUTPUT

```
123.0
```

EXPLANATION

- ≡ In this example, the float() function is used to convert the integer 123 to a floating-point number 123.0.
- ≡ The resulting floating-point number can then be used in arithmetic operations, comparisons, or stored in a variable for further processing.

int() , float() function ← CONVERTING

INTEGER , FLOAT ← CONVERTING STRING

INTEGER ← CONVERTING STRING

EXAMPLE

Using int() function.

```
# Convert a string to an integer , Using int() function
string_number = "123"
number = int(string_number)


# Print the integer value
print(number)
```

OUTPUT

```
123
```

EXPLANATION

≡ In this example, the int() function is used to convert the string "123" to an integer value 123.

≡ The resulting integer can then be used in arithmetic operations, comparisons, or stored in a variable for further processing.

FLOAT ← CONVERTING STRING

EXAMPLE

Using float() function.

This function takes a string representing a number as input and returns its floating-point representation.

```
# Get user input as a string
input_string = input("Enter a floating-point number: ")


# Convert the input string to a floating-point number ,
   Using float() function
try:
    float_number = float(input_string)


    print("Floating-point number:", float_number)
except ValueError:
    print("Invalid input. Please enter a valid floating-point
            number.")
```

OUTPUT

```
FIRST (ENTER)
Enter a floating-point number: 3.14
Floating-point number: 3.14
```

```
SECOND (ENTER)

Enter a floating-point number: abc
Invalid input. Please enter a valid floating-point number.
```

EXPLANATION

- ≡ We use the input() function to prompt the user to enter a floating-point number.
- ≡ The input is obtained as a string.

- ≡ We then use a try-except block to handle potential conversion errors.
- ≡ If the input string can be successfully converted to a floating-point number using float(), the float_number variable will contain the converted value.
- ≡ If the input is not a valid floating-point number, a ValueError will be raised, and we print an error message.

- ✓ By using the float() function, you can easily convert input strings into floating-point numbers in Python.

CHAPTER 6

OPERATORS IN PYTHON

ARITHMETIC , BITWISE , COMPARISON , LOGICAL , TERNARY

OPERATORS ← ARITHMETIC

≡ Python operators are special symbols used to perform specific operations on one or more operands.

≡ Operands ← May be variables, values, or expressions.

EXAMPLE

To add two variables, values, or expressions.

Python's addition operator (+) is used.

OPERATORS ← ARITHMETIC

≡ In Python, arithmetic operators are used to perform mathematical operations.

We will see different arithmetic operators in Python.

ADDITION (+):

Doing Addition , concatenation.

EXAMPLE

```
a = 5
b = 3
result = a + b
print("Addition:", result)
```

```
Addition: 8
```

SUBTRACTION (-):

Doing Subtraction, set difference.

EXAMPLE

```
a = 7
b = 4
result = a - b
print("Subtraction:", result)
```

OUTPUT

```
Subtraction: 3
```

MULTIPLICATION (*):

Doing Multiplication, repetition.

EXAMPLE

```
a = 6
```

```
b = 5
result = a * b
print("Multiplication:", result)
```

OUTPUT

```
Multiplication: 30
```

DIVISION (/):

Doing Division.

EXAMPLE

```
a = 10
b = 3
result = a / b
print("Division:", result)
```

OUTPUT

```
Division: 3.3333333333333335
```

FLOOR DIVISION (//):

Doing Division: true and floor.

EXAMPLE

```
a = 10
b = 3
```

```
result = a // b
print("Floor Division:", result)
```

OUTPUT

```
Floor Division: 3
```

MODULUS (%):

Doing Remainder, format.

EXAMPLE

```
a = 10
b = 3
result = a % b
print("Modulus:", result)
```

OUTPUT

```
Modulus: 1
```

OPERATORS ← BITWISE

≡ In Python, bitwise operators are used to perform bitwise operations on integers.

We will see different bitwise operators in Python.

BITWISE AND (&):

≡ Performs a bitwise AND operation on the corresponding bits of two integers.

EXAMPLE

```
a = 5  # 0101 in binary
b = 3  # 0011 in binary

result = a & b
print("Bitwise AND:", result)
```

OUTPUT

```
Bitwise AND: 1 (0001 in binary)
```

BITWISE OR (|):

≡ Performs a bitwise OR operation on the corresponding bits of two integers.

EXAMPLE

```
a = 5  # 0101 in binary
```

```
b = 3  # 0011 in binary

result = a | b
print("Bitwise OR:", result)
```

OUTPUT

```
Bitwise OR: 7 (0111 in binary)
```

BITWISE XOR (^):

≡ Performs a bitwise XOR (exclusive OR) operation on the corresponding bits of two integers.

EXAMPLE

```
a = 5  # 0101 in binary
b = 3  # 0011 in binary

result = a ^ b
print("Bitwise XOR:", result)
```

OUTPUT

```
Bitwise XOR: 6 (0110 in binary)
```

BITWISE NOT (~):

≡ Performs a bitwise NOT (complement) operation, which inverts all the bits of an integer.

EXAMPLE

```
a = 5  # 0101 in binary


result = ~a
print("Bitwise NOT:", result)
```

OUTPUT

```
Bitwise NOT: -6 (1010 in binary for 32-bit integers)
```

LEFT SHIFT (<<):

- ≡ Shifts the bits of an integer to the left by a specified number of positions, filling the shifted positions with zeros.

EXAMPLE

```
a = 5  # 0101 in binary


result = a << 2
print("Left Shift:", result)
```

OUTPUT

```
Left Shift: 20 (10100 in binary)
```

RIGHT SHIFT (>>):

≡ Shifts the bits of an integer to the right by a specified number of positions, filling the shifted positions with zeros or the sign bit (for signed integers).

EXAMPLE

```
a = 10  # 1010 in binary


result = a >> 1
print("Right Shift:", result)
```

OUTPUT

```
Right Shift: 5 (0101 in binary)
```

These examples demonstrate the use of each bitwise operator in Python.

You can experiment with different values to see how the operators behave with various inputs.

OPERATORS ← COMPARISON

≡ In Python, comparison operators are used to compare values and return Boolean results (True or False) based on the comparison.

We will see different comparison operators in Python.

EQUAL TO (==):

≡ Returns True if the operands are equal.

EXAMPLE

```
a = 5
b = 5


result = a == b
print("Is", a, "equal to", b, "?", result)
```

OUTPUT

```
Is 5 equal to 5 ? True
```

NOT EQUAL TO (!=):

≡ Returns True if the operands are not equal.

EXAMPLE

```
a = 5
b = 6
```

```
result = a != b
print("Is", a, "not equal to", b, "?", result)
```

OUTPUT

```
Is 5 not equal to 6 ? True
```

GREATER THAN (>):

≡ Returns True if the left operand is greater than the right operand.

EXAMPLE

```
a = 6
b = 5


result = a > b
print("Is", a, "greater than", b, "?", result)
```

OUTPUT

```
Is 6 greater than 5 ? True
```

LESS THAN (<):

≡ Returns True if the left operand is less than the right operand.

EXAMPLE

```
a = 5
b = 6

result = a < b
print("Is", a, "less than", b, "?", result)
```

OUTPUT

```
Is 5 less than 6 ? True
```

GREATER THAN OR EQUAL TO (>=):

≡ Returns True if the left operand is greater than or equal to the right operand.

EXAMPLE

```
a = 6
b = 6
result = a >= b
print("Is", a, "greater than or equal to", b, "?", result)
```

OUTPUT

```
Is 6 greater than or equal to 6 ? True
```

LESS THAN OR EQUAL TO (<=):

≡ Returns True if the left operand is less than or equal to the right operand.

EXAMPLE

```
a = 5
b = 6

result = a <= b
print("Is", a, "less than or equal to", b, "?", result)
```

OUTPUT

```
Is 5 less than or equal to 6 ? True
```

EXPLANATION

- ≡ These examples demonstrate the use of each comparison operator in Python.
- ≡ You can change the values of a and b to test different comparisons.
- ✓ These operators are commonly used in conditional statements, loops, and other contexts where comparison of values is needed.

OPERATORS ← LOGICAL

≡ In Python, logical operators are used to combine multiple conditions and produce a single Boolean result (True or False).

We will see different logical operators in Python.

LOGICAL AND (and):

Returns True if both operands are True.

EXAMPLE

```
a = True
b = False


result = a and b
print("Logical AND:", result)
```

OUTPUT

```
Logical AND: False
```

LOGICAL OR (or):

Returns True if at least one of the operands is True.

EXAMPLE

```
a = True
b = False
```

```
result = a or b
print("Logical OR:", result)
```

OUTPUT

```
Logical OR: True
```

LOGICAL NOT (not):

Returns True if the operand is False, and False if the operand is True.

EXAMPLE

```
a = True

result = not a
print("Logical NOT:", result)
```

OUTPUT

```
Logical NOT: False
```

EXPLANATION

- ≡ These examples demonstrate the use of each logical operator in Python.
- ≡ You can change the values of a and b to test different logical operations.
- ✓ These operators are commonly used in conditional statements, loops, and other contexts where logical operations are needed.

OPERATORS ← TERNARY

- ≡ The ternary operator in Python is a conditional expression that evaluates a condition and returns one of two values depending on whether the condition is true or false.
- ≡ It is also known as the conditional expression.

We will see ternary operators in Python.

SYNTAX

```
x = <value_if_true> if <condition> else <value_if_false>
```

Here's how the ternary operator works.

- ≡ <condition> is evaluated first. If it is true, <value_if_true> is returned; otherwise, <value_if_false> is returned.
- ≡ The ternary operator is an expression, not a statement, so it can be used within larger expressions or assignments.

EXAMPLE

```
x = 10
y = 20


max_value = x if x > y else y
print("Maximum value:", max_value)
```

OUTPUT

```
Maximum value: 20
```

EXPLANATION

- ≡ The condition $x > y$ is evaluated first. If it is true, x is assigned to max_value; otherwise, y is assigned.
- ≡ Since x (10) is not greater than y (20), the value of y (20) is assigned to max_value.
- ✓ The ternary operator makes the code concise and readable, especially in situations where you need to choose between two values based on a condition.

OPERATORS ← USING TERNARY

ASSIGNING MAXIMUM VALUE:

EXAMPLE

```
x = 10
y = 20


max_value = x if x > y else y
print("Maximum value:", max_value)
```

OUTPUT

```
Maximum value: 20
```

CHECKING EVEN OR ODD:

EXAMPLE

```
num = 15
```

```
result = "Even" if num % 2 == 0 else "Odd"
print(num, "is", result)
```

OUTPUT

```
15 is Odd
```

ASSIGNING ABSOLUTE VALUE:

EXAMPLE

```
number = -10

absolute_value = number if number >= 0 else -number
print("Absolute value:", absolute_value)
```

OUTPUT

```
Absolute value: 10
```

CHECKING FOR VALIDITY:

EXAMPLE

```
username = "john_doe"

message = "Valid" if len(username) >= 8 else "Invalid"
print("Username is", message)
```

OUTPUT

HANDLING DIVISION BY ZERO:

EXAMPLE

```
dividend = 10
divisor = 0


result = dividend / divisor if divisor != 0 else "Error: Division by Zero"
print("Result:", result)
```

OUTPUT

Result: Error: Division by Zero

CHAPTER 7

STATEMENTS IN PYTHON

If STATEMENTS , while LOOP , for LOOP

INTRODUCTION , SYNTAX , EXAMPLE

If STATEMENTS

If STATEMENTS ← INTRODUCTION

≡ In Python, the if statement is a control flow statement that allows you to execute a block of code based on whether a specified condition evaluates to True.

≡ It is used for decision-making in programming.

If STATEMENTS ← SYNTAX

```python
if condition:
    # Code block to execute if the condition is True
    statement1
    statement2
    ...
```

Here's how the if statement works.

≡ The condition is evaluated.

- If it is True, the code block following the if statement is executed.
- If it is False, the code block is skipped.

- The code block under the if statement is typically indented to indicate that it belongs to the if statement.
- The indentation is usually four spaces, but it can be any consistent whitespace.
- Optionally, you can include an else statement to specify a block of code to execute if the condition is False.
- Additionally, you can use elif (short for "else if") to specify additional conditions to check.

If STATEMENTS ← EXAMPLE

```
x = 10

if x > 5:
    print("x is greater than 5")
```

OUTPUT

```
x is greater than 5
```

EXPLANATION

- The condition x > 5 is evaluated.
- Since x is 10, which is greater than 5, the condition is True.
- Therefore, the code block under the if statement is executed, and the message "x is greater than 5" is printed to the console.

if-else STATEMENTS ← INTRODUCTION

- ≡ In Python, the if-else statement is used to execute two block of code.
- ≡ First , If condition in the if statement is true , then execute the if statement block of code.
- ≡ Second , If condition is false , then execute the else statement block of code.

if-else STATEMENTS ← SYNTAX

```
if condition:
    # Code block to execute if the condition is True
    statement1
    statement2
    ...
else:
    # Code block to execute if the condition is False
    statement3
    statement4
    ...
```

if-else STATEMENTS ← EXAMPLE

```
x = 4

if x > 5:
    print("x is greater than 5")
else:
    print ("x is less than 5")
```

OUTPUT

```
x is less than 5
```

EXPLANATION

- ≡ The condition $x > 5$ is evaluated.
- ≡ Since x is 4, which is less than 5, the condition is False.

- ≡ Therefore, the code block under the else statement is executed, and the message "x is less than 5" is printed to the console.

CHAINED if-elif-else STATEMENTS ← INTRODUCTION

- ≡ In Python, the Chained if-elif-else statement is used to check multiple block of code for True.
- ≡ And , execute a block of code as soon as one of the conditions evaluates to True.
- ≡ Similar to the else block, the elif block is also optional.
- ≡ However, a program can contains only one else block.
- ≡ Whereas there can be an a number of elif blocks following an if block.

CHAINED if-elif-else STATEMENTS ← SYNTAX

```
if condition1:
    # Code block to execute if condition1 is True
    statement1
    statement2
    ...
elif condition2:
    # Code block to execute if condition2 is True
    statement3
    statement4
    ...
elif condition3:
    # Code block to execute if condition3 is True
    statement5
```

```
    statement6

    ...
else:
    # Code block to execute if all conditions are False
    statement7
    statement8

    ...
```

CHAINED if-elif-else STATEMENTS ← EXAMPLE

```
x = 10
y = 20
if x > y:
    print("x is greater than y")
elif x < y:
    print("x is less than y")
else:
    print("x is equal to y")
```

OUTPUT

```
x is less than y
```

EXPLANATION

- ≡ In this example, we compare the values of x and y using the relational operators (>, <, ==).
- ≡ Depending on the comparison result, different messages are printed using the if, elif, and else statements.

NESTED if STATEMENTS ← INTRODUCTION

- ≡ In Python, the Nested if statement can have one or more inner if statement block of code.
- ≡ And, is used to check multiple block of code for True in inner if statement also.
- ≡ And , execute a block of code as soon as one of the conditions evaluates to True.

NESTED if STATEMENTS ← SYNTAX

```
if condition1:
   if condition2:
      # Code block to execute if both condition1 and condition2
are True
      statement1
      statement2
      ...
```

NESTED if STATEMENTS ← EXAMPLE

```
x = 20
y = 20

if x > y:
   print("x is greater than y")
```

```
    if x == y:
        print("x is equal to y")
    else:
        print("x is not equal to y")


elif x < y:
    print("x is less than y")
else:
    print("x is equal to y")
```

OUTPUT

```
x is equal to y
```

EXPLANATION

- ≡ In this example, we compare the values of x and y using the relational operators (>, <, ==).
- ≡ Depending on the comparison result, different messages are printed using the if, elif, and else statements.

while Loop

while Loop ← Introduction

- ≡ In Python, in while loop there is always some condition(expression).
- ≡ In while loop , condition is evaluated before each iteration of the loop.
- ≡ If the condition evaluates to True, the loop body is executed.
- ≡ If the condition evaluates to False, the loop terminates.

while Loop ← Syntax

```
while condition:
    # Code block to be executed repeatedly
    # as long as the condition is True
```

EXPLANATION

- ≡ In while loop , condition is an expression that is evaluated before each iteration of the loop.
- ≡ If the condition evaluates to True, the loop body is executed.
- ≡ If the condition evaluates to False, the loop terminates.
- ≡ The colon (:) at the end of the while statement indicates the start of the indented block of code that will be executed repeatedly as long as the condition is True.
- ≡ The code inside the loop block is indented to signify that it belongs to the loop body.

- ≡ The loop continues to execute the code block repeatedly until the condition becomes False.
- ≡ If the condition never becomes False, you can end up with an infinite loop.

while LOOP ← EXAMPLE

```
i = 0
while i < 5:
    print(i)
    if i == 2:
        break
    i += 1
```

OUTPUT

```
0
1
2
```

EXPLANATION

In this example, the loop terminates prematurely when i becomes equal to 2 due to the break statement.

for LOOP

for LOOP ← INTRODUCTION

- ≡ In Python, a for loop is used to iterate over a sequence (such as a list, tuple, string, or range) or any iterable object.
- ≡ The for loop executes a block of code multiple times, once for each item in the sequence or iterable.

for LOOP ← SYNTAX

```
for item in sequence:
    # Code block to be executed for each item in the sequence
```

EXPLANATION

- ≡ item is a variable that takes on the value of each item in the sequence during each iteration of the loop.
- ≡ sequence is the sequence of elements over which the loop iterates. It can be any iterable object, such as a list, tuple, string, or range.
- ≡ The colon (:) at the end of the for statement indicates the start of the indented block of code that will be executed for each item in the sequence.
- ≡ The code inside the loop block is indented to signify that it belongs to the loop body.
- ≡ During each iteration of the loop, the item variable takes on the value of the next element in the sequence, and the code block inside the loop is executed with that value.

for LOOP ← EXAMPLE

Using a for loop to iterate over a list.

```
fruits = ["apple", "banana", "cherry"]
for fruit in fruits:
    print(fruit)
```

OUTPUT

```
apple
banana
cherry
```

EXPLANATION

In this example, the for loop iterates over each item in the fruits list, and during each iteration, the fruit variable takes on the value of the current item, which is then printed.

CHAPTER 8

STATEMENTS IN PYTHON

break STATEMENTS , continue STATEMENTS

IN

for LOOP , while LOOP

INTRODUCTION , SYNTAX , EXAMPLE

break STATEMENTS ← INTRODUCTION

- ≡ In Python, the break statement is used to exit (or "break out of") a loop prematurely.
- ≡ When a break statement is encountered inside a loop (such as a for loop or a while loop).
- ≡ The loop is immediately terminated.

continue STATEMENTS ← INTRODUCTION

- ≡ In Python, the continue statement is used inside loops (such as for loops and while loops).
- ≡ To skip the rest of the code inside the loop for the current iteration and continue with the next iteration of the loop.

for LOOP

for LOOP ← break STATEMENTS ← SYNTAX

```
for item in iterable:
    # Code block
    if condition:
        break
```

EXPLANATION

- ≡ The break statement is used to exit the loop immediately when a certain condition is met.
- ≡ It can be placed inside a conditional statement (if statement) to define the condition under which the loop should be terminated.
- ≡ Once the break statement is executed, the loop is terminated. And the program execution continues from the statement immediately following the loop.

for LOOP ← continue STATEMENTS ← SYNTAX

```
for item in iterable:
    # Code block
    if condition:
        continue
    # More code
```

EXPLANATION

- ≡ iterable is the sequence or iterable object over which the loop iterates in the case of a for loop or condition.
- ≡ The if statement with condition inside the loop block checks if a certain condition is met.

- ≡ If the condition evaluates to True, the continue statement is executed.
- ≡ Causing the rest of the code inside the loop for the current iteration to be skipped, and the loop proceeds to the next iteration.

for LOOP ← break STATEMENTS ← EXAMPLE

```
for i in range(5):
    print(i)
    if i == 2:
        break
```

OUTPUT

```
0
1
2
```

EXPLANATION

- ≡ In this example, the loop iterates over the range from 0 to 4.
- ≡ When i becomes equal to 2.

- ≡ if condition i == 2 becomes true, and the break statement is executed.

- ≡ As a result, the loop is terminated prematurely, and the program execution continues after the loop.
- ✓ The break statement is often used in combination with conditional statements (if statements) inside loops to exit.
- ✓ The loop based on certain conditions.

- ✓ It provides a way to terminate the loop prematurely when a specific condition is met.
- ✓ Which can be useful for optimization or for handling special cases.

for LOOP ← continue STATEMENTS ← EXAMPLE

```
for i in range(5):
  if i == 2:
    continue
  print(i)
```

OUTPUT

```
0
1
3
4
```

EXPLANATION

- ≡ In this example, when i becomes equal to 2, the continue statement is executed.
- ≡ The rest of the code inside the loop for that iteration (i.e., print(i)) is skipped.
- ≡ The loop proceeds to the next iteration.

while LOOP

while LOOP ← break STATEMENTS ← SYNTAX

```
while condition:
    # Code block
    if condition:
        break
```

EXPLANATION

- ≡ condition is the expression that determines whether the loop should continue executing or not.
- ≡ The while loop continues to execute as long as the condition evaluates to True.
- ≡ Inside the loop block, the if statement with condition checks if a certain condition is met.

- ≡ If the condition evaluates to True, the break statement is executed, causing the loop to terminate immediately.
- ≡ The program execution continues from the statement immediately following the loop.

while LOOP ← continue STATEMENTS ← SYNTAX

```
while condition:
    # Code block
    if condition:
```

```
        continue
    # More code
```

EXPLANATION

- ≡ condition is the expression that determines whether the loop should continue executing.
- ≡ The while loop continues to execute as long as the condition evaluates to True.
- ≡ Inside the loop block, the if statement with condition checks if a certain condition is met.

- ≡ If the condition evaluates to True, the continue statement is executed.
- ≡ Causing the rest of the code inside the loop for the current iteration to be skipped.
- ≡ The loop proceeds to the next iteration.

while LOOP ← break STATEMENTS ← EXAMPLE

```
i = 0
while i < 5:
    print(i)
    if i == 2:
        break
    i += 1
```

OUTPUT

```
0
1
2
```

EXPLANATION

≡ In this example, the loop terminates prematurely when i
   becomes equal to 2 due to the break statement.

while LOOP ← continue STATEMENTS ← EXAMPLE

```
i = 0
while i < 5:
    i += 1
    if i == 3:
        continue
    print(i)
```

OUTPUT

```
1
2
4
5
```

EXPLANATION

- ≡ In this example, when i becomes equal to 3, the continue statement is executed.
- ≡ Causing the rest of the code inside the loop for that iteration to be skipped.
- ≡ The loop proceeds to the next iteration, and the remaining values of i are printed.

CHAPTER 9

FUNCTION IN PYTHON

FUNCTION ← INTRODUCTION

- ≡ In Python, a function is a block of reusable code that performs a specific task.
- ≡ Functions provide a way to organize code into manageable pieces, improve code reusability, and make the code more readable.

FUNCTION ← DEFINING

EXAMPLE

```
def function_name(parameter1, parameter2, ...):
    # Function body
    # Code to perform the task
    return result
```

EXPLANATION

- ≡ def keyword is used to define a function.
- ≡ function_name is the name of the function.
- ≡ (parameter1, parameter2, ...) is the list of parameters (if any) that the function accepts. Parameters are optional.

- ≡ : colon indicates the beginning of the function body.
- ≡ The function body consists of the code that performs the task.
- ≡ return result statement (optional) is used to return a value from the function. If there's no return statement, the function returns None by default.

FUNCTION ← USING FUNCTION

```
result = function_name(argument1, argument2, ...)
```

EXPLANATION

- ≡ function_name is the name of the function to call.
- ≡ (argument1, argument2, ...) is the list of arguments (if any) to pass to the function. Arguments are optional.
- ≡ The function is called with the specified arguments, and the result (if any) is stored in the result variable.

EXAMPLE

```
# Function definition
def add_numbers(x, y):
    # Function body: adds two numbers
    result = x + y
    return result

# Using the function
```

```
sum_result = add_numbers(3, 5)
print("Sum:", sum_result)
```

OUTPUT

```
Sum: 8
```

EXPLANATION

- ≡ We define a function add_numbers that takes two parameters x and y, adds them together, and returns the result.
- ≡ We call the function add_numbers with arguments 3 and 5, and store the result in the variable sum_result.
- ≡ We print the result to the console.

FUNCTION : PARAMETERS

FUNCTION ← INTRODUCTION

- ≡ In Python, function parameters are variables that are specified in the function definition and are used to pass values to the function when it is called.
- ≡ Parameters allow functions to accept input values and perform operations on them.

FUNCTION ← DEFINING PARAMETERS

```
def function_name(parameter1, parameter2, ...):
    # Function body
    # Code that uses parameter1, parameter2, ...
```

EXPLANATION

- ≡ def keyword is used to define a function.
- ≡ function_name is the name of the function.
- ≡ (parameter1, parameter2, ...) is the list of parameters that the function accepts. Parameters are optional.
- ≡ Each parameter in the list is a variable that holds the value passed to the function.
- ≡ Parameters are separated by commas.

FUNCTION ← USING PARAMETERS

```
result = function_name(argument1, argument2, ...)
```

EXPLANATION

- ≡ function_name is the name of the function to call.
- ≡ (argument1, argument2, ...) is the list of arguments that are passed to the function. Arguments are optional.
- ≡ Arguments are the actual values that are passed to the function when it is called.
- ≡ The function uses these arguments to perform its task.

EXAMPLE

```
# Function definition with parameters
def greet(name):
    # Function body: greets the user with the provided name
    print("Hello,", name, "!")
# Using the function with an argument
greet("Alice")
```

OUTPUT

```
Hello, Alice!
```

EXPLANATION

- ≡ We define a function greet that takes a single parameter name.
- ≡ When the function is called with the argument "Alice", the value "Alice" is passed to the parameter name.
- ≡ Inside the function, the parameter name holds the value "Alice", and the function prints "Hello, Alice!" to the console.

FUNCTION : PARAMETERS KEYWORDS

FUNCTION ← PARAMETERS KEYWORDS

- ≡ Keyword parameters (also known as keyword arguments) in Python are parameters that are passed to a function by specifying their corresponding parameter names along with the values.
- ≡ Keyword parameters allow you to provide arguments to a function in any order, making the function call more readable and flexible.

FUNCTION ← DEFINING PARAMETERS KEYWORDS

```
def function_name(param1=default_value1,
param2=default_value2, ...):

    # Function body

    # Code that uses param1, param2, ...
```

EXPLANATION

- ≡ def keyword is used to define a function.
- ≡ function_name is the name of the function.
- ≡ (param1=default_value1, param2=default_value2, ...) is the list of parameters with their default values (if any). Keyword parameters are optional.
- ≡ Each parameter in the list is defined with its default value using the syntax param=default_value.
- ≡ Default values are used if no value is provided for the corresponding parameter during the function call.

FUNCTION ← USING PARAMETERS KEYWORDS

```
result = function_name(param1=value1, param2=value2, ...)
```

EXPLANATION

- ≡ function_name is the name of the function to call.
- ≡ param1=value1, param2=value2, etc., are the keyword arguments passed to the function.
- ≡ Each keyword argument consists of the parameter name followed by the value assigned to it.
- ≡ Keyword arguments can be provided in any order.

EXAMPLE

```python
# Function definition with keyword parameters
def greet(name, message="Hello"):
    # Function body: greets the user with the provided name and message
    print(message, name, "!")


# Using the function with keyword arguments
greet(message="Hi", name="Bob")
```

OUTPUT

```
Hi Bob!
```

EXPLANATION

- ≡ We define a function greet that takes two parameters: name and message.
- ≡ The parameter message has a default value "Hello".
- ≡ When the function is called with keyword arguments message="Hi" and name="Bob", these arguments are passed to the corresponding parameters.
- ≡ The function uses the provided values to print the greeting message "Hi Bob!" to the console.

FUNCTION : DEFAULT , RETURN VALUE

FUNCTION ← DEFAULT VALUE ← SYNTAX

≡ In Python, you can add default values to function parameters by specifying the default values directly in the function definition.

```
def function_name(param1=default_value1,
param2=default_value2, ...):
    # Function body
    # Code that uses param1, param2, ...
```

EXPLANATION

≡ param1=default_value1, param2=default_value2, etc., are the parameters with their corresponding default values.

≡ If no value is provided for a parameter during the function call, the default value specified in the function definition is used.

EXAMPLE

```
# Function definition with default parameter values
def greet(name, message="Hello"):
    # Function body: greets the user with the provided name and message
    print(message, name, "!")
```

```
# Using the function without providing the default parameter
value
greet("Alice")


# Using the function with providing a custom parameter value
greet("Bob", "Hi")
```

OUTPUT

```
Hello Alice!
Hi Bob!
```

EXPLANATION

- ≡ We define a function greet with two parameters: name and message.
- ≡ The parameter message has a default value "Hello".
- ≡ When the function is called without providing a value for the message parameter (greet("Alice")), the default value "Hello" is used, and the function prints "Hello Alice!".
- ≡ When the function is called with a custom value for the message parameter (greet("Bob", "Hi")), the provided value "Hi" is used instead of the default value, and the function prints "Hi Bob!".

FUNCTION ← RETURN VALUE ← SYNTAX

- ≡ In Python, you can return values from a function using the return statement.
- ≡ The return statement is used to exit the function and specify the value(s) that the function should return to the caller.

```
def function_name(parameter1, parameter2, ...):
    # Function body
    # Code that performs the task
    return value1, value2, ...
```

EXPLANATION

- ≡ def keyword is used to define a function.
- ≡ function_name is the name of the function.
- ≡ (parameter1, parameter2, ...) is the list of parameters that the function accepts. Parameters are optional.
- ≡ The return statement is used to exit the function and return one or more values to the caller.
- ≡ value1, value2, ... are the values that the function returns. You can return multiple values separated by commas, or a single value.

EXAMPLE

```
# Function definition with parameters and return statement
def add_numbers(x, y):
    # Function body: adds two numbers
```

```
    result = x + y
    return result


# Using the function and storing the returned value
sum_result = add_numbers(3, 5)
print("Sum:", sum_result)
```

OUTPUT

```
Sum: 8
```

EXPLANATION

- ≡ We define a function add_numbers that takes two parameters x and y, adds them together, and returns the result using the return statement.
- ≡ When the function is called with arguments 3 and 5, the function calculates the sum (3 + 5 = 8) and returns the result 8.
- ≡ The returned value is stored in the variable sum_result, and we print it to the console.

CHAPTER 10

INTRODUCTION

DATA STRUCTURES

LIST , TUPLE , DICTIONARY , SET

LIST ← INTRODUCTION

- ≡ In Python, a list is a built-in data structure that represents a collection of items in a specific order.
- ≡ Lists are mutable, meaning that you can modify their elements after they have been created.
- ≡ Lists can contain elements of different data types, and they can grow or shrink dynamically as needed.

Here's a simple example of a Python list:

EXAMPLE

```python
# Creating a list
my_list = [1, 2, 3, 4, 5]


# Accessing elements of the list
print(my_list[0])                    # Output: 1
```

```python
print(my_list[2])                      # Output: 3

# Modifying elements of the list
my_list[1] = 10
print(my_list)                         # Output: [1, 10, 3, 4, 5]

# Adding elements to the list
my_list.append(6)
print(my_list)                         # Output: [1, 10, 3, 4, 5, 6]

# Removing elements from the list
my_list.remove(3)
print(my_list)                         # Output: [1, 10, 4, 5, 6]
```

You might need to use a list in Python when.

STORING MULTIPLE VALUES:

You need to store multiple values of possibly different data types in a single variable.

MAINTAINING ORDER:

You need to preserve the order of elements in the collection.

DYNAMIC SIZE:

You need a data structure that can dynamically grow or shrink as elements are added or removed.

MUTABLE OPERATIONS:

You need to perform mutable operations such as adding, removing, or modifying elements in the collection.

INDEXING AND SLICING:

You need to access elements by their index or perform slicing operations to extract subsets of elements.

- ✓ Lists are incredibly versatile and are widely used in Python programming for tasks such as storing collections of items, representing sequences of data, managing sets of values, and more.
- ✓ They provide a flexible and efficient way to work with collections of data in Python.

TUPLE ← INTRODUCTION

- ≡ A Python tuple is an immutable, ordered collection of elements.
- ≡ Immutable means that once a tuple is created, its elements cannot be changed or modified.
- ≡ Tuples are similar to lists, but they are enclosed in parentheses () instead of square brackets [].

You can create a tuple in Python by enclosing elements within parentheses ().

Here are a few examples of creating tuples.

EXAMPLE

```python
# Creating an empty tuple
empty_tuple = ()


# Creating a tuple with elements
my_tuple = (1, 2, 3, 4, 5)


# Creating a tuple with elements of different types
mixed_tuple = (1, "apple", 3.14, True)


# Creating a single-element tuple (note the comma)
single_element_tuple = (42,)
```

```
# You can also create a tuple without parentheses (not
  recommended for readability)
another_tuple = 1, 2, 3
```

- ✓ Tuples are commonly used for grouping data that belongs
  together, like coordinates, records from a database, or
  returning multiple values from a function.
- ✓ Because tuples are immutable, they provide a certain level
  of safety when dealing with data that should not be changed
  accidentally.

DICTIONARY ← INTRODUCTION

- ≡ A Python dictionary is an unordered collection of key-value
  pairs.
- ≡ Each key in a dictionary is unique and immutable, and it
  maps to a corresponding value.
- ≡ You can think of a dictionary like a real-world dictionary,
  where each word (key) has a definition (value).

You can create a dictionary in Python using curly braces {} and
specifying key-value pairs separated by colons : .

Here's how you can create a dictionary.

EXAMPLE

```
# Creating an empty dictionary
empty_dict = {}
```

```
# Creating a dictionary with key-value pairs
my_dict = {'name': 'John', 'age': 30, 'city': 'New York'}


# Creating a dictionary using the dict() constructor
another_dict = dict(name='Alice', age=25, city='Los Angeles')
```

- ≡ empty_dict is an empty dictionary.
- ≡ my_dict contains three key-value pairs: 'name': 'John', 'age': 30, and 'city': 'New York'.
- ≡ another_dict is created using the dict() constructor, where keys and values are specified as keyword arguments.

- ✓ You can access, modify, add, or remove elements from a dictionary using its keys.
- ✓ Dictionaries are widely used for storing and retrieving data efficiently, especially when you need to access values by their associated keys.

SET ← INTRODUCTION

- ≡ In Python, a set is an unordered collection of unique elements.
- ≡ Unlike lists or tuples, sets do not allow duplicate values i.e. each element in a set must be unique.

- ✓ Sets are mutable, meaning you can add or remove items after a set has been created.
- ✓ Sets are defined using curly braces {} or the built-in set() function.

Here's how you can create a set.

EXAMPLE

```python
# Creating a set
my_set = {1, 2, 3, 4, 5}


# Accessing elements of the set
my_set = {1, 2, 3, 4, 5}
for my_set1 in my_set:
  print (my_set1)


# Adding elements to the set
my_set = {1, 2, 3, 3}
my_set.add(4)
print(my_set)  # Output: {1, 2, 3, 4}
```

```
# Removing elements from the set
my_set = {1, 2, 3, 4}
my_set.remove(3)
print(my_set)   # Output: {1, 2, 4}
```

≡ You can create set within curly braces, separating each element by a comma.

≡ You can access set items is by traversing the set using a loop, such as a for loop.

≡ By iterating over the set, you can access each element one by one

≡ And perform operations on them as needed.

≡ You can add an element to a set.

≡ You can use the add() function.

≡ This is useful when you want to include new elements into an existing set.

≡ You can remove an element from a set using the remove() function. This is useful when you want to eliminate specific elements from the set.

CHAPTER 11

ADDING , INSERTING , ACCESSING ,
MODIFYING , REMOVING ELEMENTS
IN
DATA STRUCTURES
LIST , TUPLE , DICTIONARY , SET

DATA STRUCTURES : ADDING

LIST ← ADDING ELEMENTS

≡ To add elements to a Python list, you can use append()
method.

USING append() METHOD:

≡ The append() method adds a single element to the end of
the list.

EXAMPLE

```python
# Define a list
my_list = ['apple', 'banana', 'cherry']

# Add a single element to the end of the list
my_list.append('date')

# Print the modified list
print(my_list)
```

OUTPUT

```
['apple', 'banana', 'cherry', 'date']
```

EXPLANATION

- ≡ In example, we first define a list (my_list).
- ≡ Then, we use the methods append() to add elements to the list.
- ≡ Finally, we print the modified list to verify the changes.

- ✓ Here methods provide flexible ways to add elements to a list in Python.
- ✓ Allowing you to easily extend the list with new data as needed.

TUPLE ← ADDING ELEMENTS

≡ To add elements to a Python tuple, you can use append() method.

≡ The append() function is used to add a single element to the end of a list.

≡ However, since tuples are immutable, the append() function cannot be directly used to update a tuple.

✓ To update a tuple using the append() function.
✓ We need to first convert the tuple to a list.
✓ Then use append() to add elements.
✓ And finally convert the list back to a tuple.

EXAMPLE

```
# Original tuple , Before Adding New Element To tuple
my_tuple1 = (1, 2, 3)


# Converting tuple to list
my_list_my_tuple1 = list(my_tuple1)


# New Element to be added
new_elements = [4, 5, 6]


# Updating the list using append()
```

```
for element in new_elements:
    my_list_my_tuple1.append(element)

# Converting list back to tuple
updated_my_tuple2 = tuple(my_list_my_tuple1)

# Printing the updated tuple, After Adding New Element To
    tuple

print("Original tuple , Before Adding New Element To tuple:",
    my_tuple1)

print("New Element To be Added To , tuple:", new_elements)

print("updated tuple, After Adding New Element To tuple:",

    updated_my_tuple2)
```

OUTPUT

```
Original tuple , Before Adding New Element To tuple:
(1, 2, 3)

New Element To be Added To , tuple: [4, 5, 6]
```

updated tuple, After Adding New Element To tuple:
(1, 2, 3, 4, 5, 6)

EXPLANATION

- ≡ In this example, first we will convert the original tuple "my_tuple1(1, 2, 3)" to a list "my_list_my_tuple1[1, 2, 3]".

- ≡ Second , New Element to be added [4, 5, 6] to list.

- ≡ We then use a loop (for loop) to iterate over the new elements and append each one to the list using the append() function.

- ≡ Next , we convert the updated list (my_list_my_tuple1) back to a tuple (updated_my_tuple2) to get the updated tuple (updated_my_tuple2) , (1, 2, 3, 4, 5, 6) .

DICTIONARY ← ADDING ELEMENTS

- ≡ Adding a new key-value pair to a Python dictionary is straightforward.
- ≡ You can do it by assigning a value to a new key like this.

EXAMPLE

```python
# Create a dictionary
my_dict = {'a': 1, 'b': 2}


# Add a new key-value pair
my_dict['c'] = 3


print(my_dict)
```

OUTPUT

```
{'a': 1, 'b': 2, 'c': 3}
```

EXPLANATION

In this example, the key 'c' is added with the value 3.

You can add any key-value pair in a similar manner.

SET ← ADDING ELEMENTS

≡ To add elements to a Python set, you can use various methods such as add(), update().

Here's how you can add elements to a set using these methods.

EXAMPLE

```
# Define a set
my_set = {1, 2, 3, 3}

# Add a single element to the end of the set
my_set.add(4)


# Print the modified set
print(my_set)
```

OUTPUT

```
{1, 2, 3, 4}
```

EXPLANATION

≡ In example, we first define a set (my_set).
≡ Then, we use the methods add () to add elements to the set.
≡ Finally, we print the modified my_set to verify the changes.
✓ Here methods provide flexible ways to add elements to a set in Python.
✓ Allowing you to easily extend the set with new data as needed.

DATA STRUCTURES : INSERTING

LIST ← INSERTING ELEMENTS

- ≡ To insert elements in the middle of a Python list, you can use the insert() method.
- ≡ The insert() method allows you to specify the index where you want to insert the new element.

Here's how you can insert elements into the middle of a list.

EXAMPLE

```
# Define a list
my_list = ['apple', 'banana', 'cherry', 'date']


# Insert an element in the middle of the list
# Insert 'blueberry' at index 2
my_list.insert(2, 'blueberry')


# Print the modified list
print(my_list)
```

OUTPUT

```
['apple', 'banana', 'blueberry', 'cherry', 'date']
```

EXPLANATION

- ≡ We define a list my_list containing four elements.

- ≡ We use the insert() method to insert the element 'blueberry' at index 2.
- ≡ The index **2** indicates that the new element will be inserted after the second element ('banana') and before the third element ('cherry').
- ≡ We print the modified list to verify the changes.

- ✓ The insert() method modifies the original list in place by shifting existing elements to make room for the new element.
- ✓ It's a convenient way to insert elements at specific positions within a list.

TUPLE ← INSERTING ELEMENTS

≡ To insert new elements to a Python tuple, you can use append() method.

≡ The append() function is used to add a single element to the end of a list.

≡ However, since tuples are immutable, the append() function cannot be directly used to update a tuple.

✓ To insert new elements a tuple using the append() function.
✓ We need to first convert the tuple to a list.
✓ Then use append() to insert new elements elements.
✓ And finally convert the list back to a tuple.

EXAMPLE

```
# Original tuple , Before Inserting New Element To tuple
my_tuple1 = (1, 2, 3)


# Converting tuple to list
my_list_my_tuple1 = list(my_tuple1)


# New Element to be Inserted
new_elements = [4, 5, 6]


# Updating the list using append()
```

```
for element in new_elements:
    my_list_my_tuple1.append(element)

# Converting list back to tuple
updated_my_tuple2 = tuple(my_list_my_tuple1)

# Printing the updated tuple, After Adding New Element To
    tuple

print("Original tuple , Before Inserting New Element To
        tuple:",   my_tuple1)

print("New Element To be Inserted To , tuple:",
        new_elements)

print("Updated tuple, After Inserting New Element To tuple:",

        updated_my_tuple2)
```

OUTPUT

```
Original tuple , Before Inserting New Element To tuple:
(1, 2, 3)
```

New Element To be Inserted To , tuple: [4, 5, 6]

Updated tuple, After Inserting New Element To tuple:
(1, 2, 3, 4, 5, 6)

EXPLANATION

- ≡ In this example, first we will convert the original tuple "my_tuple1(1, 2, 3)" to a list "my_list_my_tuple1[1, 2, 3]".

- ≡ Second , New Element to be added [4, 5, 6] to list.

- ≡ We then use a loop (for loop) to iterate over the new elements and append each one to the list using the append() function.

- ≡ Next , we convert the updated list (my_list_my_tuple1) back to a tuple (updated_my_tuple2) to get the updated tuple (updated_my_tuple2) , (1, 2, 3, 4, 5, 6) .

DICTIONARY ← INSERTING ELEMENTS

- ≡ Insert a new key-value pair to a Python dictionary is straightforward.
- ≡ You can do it by assigning a value to a new key like this.

EXAMPLE

```python
# Create a dictionary
my_dict = {'a': 1, 'b': 2}


# Insert a new key-value pair
my_dict['c'] = 3


print(my_dict)
```

OUTPUT

```
{'a': 1, 'b': 2, 'c': 3}
```

EXPLANATION

In this example, the key 'c' is insert with the value 3.

You can add any key-value pair in a similar manner.

SET ← INSERTING ELEMENTS

- ≡ To insert elements to a Python set, you can use add() methods.

Here's how you can insert elements to a set using add() methods.

EXAMPLE

```
# Define a set
my_set = {1, 2, 3, 3}

# Inserting a single element to the end of the set
my_set.add(4)

# Print the modified set
print(my_set)
```

OUTPUT

```
{1, 2, 3, 4}
```

EXPLANATION

- ≡ In example, we first define a set (my_set).
- ≡ Then, we use the method add () to insert elements to the set.
- ≡ Finally, we print the modified my_set to verify the changes.
- ✓ Here methods provide flexible ways to insert elements to a set in Python.
- ✓ Allowing you to easily extend the set with new data as needed.

Data Structures : Accessing

List ← Accessing Elements By Index

- ≡ In Python, you can access elements in a list by their index.
- ≡ List indexing starts at 0, meaning the first element of the list has an index of 0, the second element has an index of 1, and so on.

- ≡ You can also use negative indices to access elements from the end of the list, where -1 represents the last element, -2 represents the second-to-last element, and so forth.

Here's how you can access elements by index in a Python list.

Example

```
# Define a list
my_list = ['apple', 'banana', 'cherry', 'date', 'elderberry']


# Access elements by index
print(my_list[0])      # Output: 'apple' (first element)
print(my_list[2])      # Output: 'cherry' (third element)
print(my_list[-1])     # Output: 'elderberry' (last element)
print(my_list[-2])     # Output: 'date' (second-to-last element)
```

Explanation

- ≡ We define a list my_list containing five elements.

- ≡ We use square brackets [] to access elements by their index within the list.
- ≡ Positive indices refer to elements starting from the beginning of the list, while negative indices refer to elements starting from the end of the list.
- ≡ We print the values of the elements at index 0, 2, -1, and -2 to demonstrate accessing elements by index.

TUPLE ← ACCESSING ELEMENTS

- ≡ Accessing elements of a tuple in Python is similar to accessing elements of other sequences like lists.
- ≡ You can use indexing to access individual elements or slicing to access multiple elements.

Here's how you can do it.

EXAMPLE

```
# Define a tuple
my_tuple = (1, 2, 3, 4, 5)


# Accessing individual elements using indexing
first_element = my_tuple[0]
second_element = my_tuple[1]
last_element = my_tuple[-1]


# Printing individual elements using indexing
```

```
print("First element:", first_element)

print("Second element:", second_element)

print("Last element:", last_element)
```

OUTPUT

```
First element: 1

Second element: 2

Last element: 5
```

EXPLANATION

- ≡ We define a list my_tuple containing five elements.
- ≡ We use square brackets [] to access elements by their index within the tuple.
- ≡ Positive indices refer to elements starting from the beginning of the tuple, while negative indices refer to elements starting from the end of the tuple.
- ≡ We print the values of the elements at index 0, 1, -1 to demonstrate accessing elements by index.

DICTIONARY ← ACCESSING ELEMENTS

≡ You can access values in a Python dictionary using the keys as indices.

Here are a few methods to access values in a dictionary.

USING SQUARE BRACKETS []:

EXAMPLE

```
my_dict = {'name': 'John', 'age': 30, 'city': 'New York'}


# Accessing values using keys
name = my_dict['name']
age = my_dict['age']
city = my_dict['city']


print("Name:", name)
print("Age:", age)
print("City:", city)
```

OUTPUT

```
Name: John
Age: 30
City: New York
```

USING THE get() METHOD:

EXAMPLE

```python
my_dict = {'name': 'John', 'age': 30, 'city': 'New York'}
# Accessing values using get() method
name = my_dict.get('name')
age = my_dict.get('age')
city = my_dict.get('city')


print("Name:", name)
print("Age:", age)
print("City:", city)
```

OUTPUT

```
Name: John
Age: 30
City: New York
```

EXPLANATION

≡ In both examples, we access the values in the dictionary my_dict using the keys 'name', 'age', and 'city'.

≡ Using square brackets is straightforward and raises a KeyError if the key is not found in the dictionary.

≡ Using the get() method allows you to provide a default value if the key is not found, which can help avoid KeyError exceptions.

SET ← ACCESSING ELEMENTS

- ≡ You can access set items is by traversing the set using a loop , such as a for loop.
- ≡ By iterating over the set, you can access each element one by one and perform operations on them as needed.

- ≡ In Python, sets are unordered collections of unique elements.
- ≡ Sets do not have a positional index for their elements.
- ≡ This means that you cannot access individual elements of a set directly by specifying an index.

EXAMPLE

```python
# Define a set
my_set = {1, 2, 3, 4}


# Accessing element of the set
for my_set1 in my_set:


# Print the elements of set
print(my_set1)
```

OUTPUT

```
1
2
3
```

EXPLANATION

- In example, we first define a set (my_set).
- Then, we will traverse the set using a loop , such as a for loop.
- By iterating over the set, we will access each element one by one of the set.
- Finally, we print the elements of my_set to one by one.

DATA STRUCTURES : MODIFYING

LIST ← MODIFYING ELEMENTS

- ≡ To modify elements in a Python list, you can directly assign new values to specific elements using their indices.
- ≡ Lists in Python are mutable, which means you can change their elements after they have been created.

Here's how you can modify elements in a Python list.

EXAMPLE

```python
# Define a list
my_list = ['apple', 'banana', 'cherry', 'date', 'elderberry']

# Modify elements in the list
my_list[1] = 'blueberry'    # Modify the element at index 1
my_list[-2] = 'grape'       # Modify the second-to-last element

# Print the modified list
print(my_list)
```

OUTPUT

```
['apple', 'blueberry', 'cherry', 'grape', 'elderberry']
```

EXPLANATION

- ≡ We define a list my_list containing five elements.

- ≡ We use square brackets [] to access elements by their indices within the list.
- ≡ We assign new values to elements at specific indices to modify them.
- ≡ We print the modified list to verify the changes.

- ✓ You can modify elements in a list using any valid Python expression.
- ✓ This means you can assign new values of the same type, different types, or even the result of an expression involving other elements in the list.
- ✓ Lists provide a flexible and powerful way to manage collections of data in Python.

TUPLE ← MODIFYING ELEMENTS

- ≡ Tuples are immutable which means you cannot update or change the values of tuple elements.
- ≡ You are able to take portions of existing tuples to create new tuples.

EXAMPLE

```
# First tuple , my_tuple1
my_tuple1 = (1, 2, 3)


# Second tuple , my_tuple2
my_tuple2 = (4, 5, 6)
```

```
# Creating New tuple , my_new_tuple
my_new_tuple = my_tuple1 + my_tuple2


# Printing New tuple , my_new_tuple
print ("Newly Created tuple:", my_new_tuple)
```

OUTPUT

```
Newly Created tuple: (1, 2, 3, 4, 5, 6)
```

DICTIONARY ← MODIFYING ELEMENTS

≡ To modify values in a Python dictionary, you can simply access the key and assign a new value to it.

Here's how you can do it.

EXAMPLE

```
# Create a dictionary
my_dict = {'a': 1, 'b': 2, 'c': 3}


# Modify the value associated with the key 'b'
my_dict['b'] = 5


print(my_dict)
```

OUTPUT

```
{'a': 1, 'b': 5, 'c': 3}
```

EXPLANATION

- ≡ In this example, the value associated with the key 'b' is modified from 2 to 5.
- ≡ You can modify the values for any key in a similar manner.

SET ← MODIFYING ELEMENTS

- ≡ To update elements to a Python set, you can use update() methods.

Here's how you can update elements to a set using update() methods.

EXAMPLE

```python
# Define a set
my_set = {1, 2, 3}

# updating a single element to the end of the set
my_set.update({4})

# Print the modified updated set
print(my_set)
```

OUTPUT

```
{1, 2, 3, 4}
```

EXPLANATION

- ≡ In example, we first define a set (my_set).
- ≡ Then, we use the method update() to update elements to the set.
- ≡ Finally, we print the modified my_set to verify the changes.

- ✓ Here methods provide flexible ways to update elements to a set in Python.
- ✓ Allowing you to easily extend the set with new data as needed.

DATA STRUCTURES : REMOVING

LIST ← REMOVING ELEMENTS BY INDEX

USING THE pop() METHOD:

- ≡ The pop() method removes and returns the element at the specified index.
- ≡ If no index is specified, it removes and returns the last element of the list.

EXAMPLE

```python
# Define a list
my_list = ['apple', 'banana', 'cherry', 'date']

# Remove and return the element at index 2
removed_element = my_list.pop(2)

# Print the modified list and the removed element
print("Modified list:", my_list)
print("Removed element:", removed_element)
```

OUTPUT

```
Modified list: ['apple', 'banana', 'date']
Removed element: 'cherry'
```

USING THE del STATEMENT:

- ≡ The del statement removes the element at the specified index from the list.
- ≡ It does not return the removed element.

EXAMPLE

```python
# Define a list
my_list = ['apple', 'banana', 'cherry', 'date']

# Remove the element at index 1
del my_list[1]

# Print the modified list
print("Modified list:", my_list)
```

OUTPUT

```
Modified list: ['apple', 'cherry', 'date']
```

EXPLANATION

- ≡ In both examples, we first define a list my_list containing elements.
- ≡ Then, we use either the pop() method or the del statement to remove an element at a specific index from the list.
- ≡ Finally, we print the modified list to verify the changes.
- ✓ Choose the method that best fits your needs based on whether you need to retrieve the removed element (pop()) or simply remove it (del).

LIST ← REMOVING ELEMENTS BY VALUE

- ≡ To remove elements from a Python list by their value, you can use the remove() method.
- ≡ The remove() method removes the first occurrence of the specified value from the list.

Here's how you can remove elements by value from a list using the remove() method.

EXAMPLE

```python
# Define a list
my_list = ['apple', 'banana', 'cherry', 'date', 'banana']


# Remove the first occurrence of the value 'banana'
my_list.remove('banana')


# Print the modified list
print("Modified list:", my_list)
```

OUTPUT

```
Modified list: ['apple', 'cherry', 'date', 'banana']
```

EXPLANATION

- ≡ We define a list my_list containing elements, including multiple occurrences of the value 'banana'.
- ≡ We use the remove() method to remove the first occurrence of the value 'banana' from the list.

- ≡ The method modifies the original list by removing the specified value.
- ≡ We print the modified list to verify the changes.

- ✓ It's important to note that if the specified value is not found in the list, the remove() method will raise a ValueError.
- ✓ Therefore, it's a good practice to ensure that the value exists in the list before attempting to remove it, or handle the ValueError using a try-except block if necessary.

TUPLE ← REMOVING ELEMENTS

- ≡ In Python, tuples are immutable, which means you cannot change the elements of a tuple once it's created.

- ≡ Therefore, there's no direct way to clear a tuple like you would with a list using the clear() method.

However, you can achieve a similar effect by creating a new empty tuple.

Here's how you can do it.

EXAMPLE

```
# Define a tuple
my_tuple = (1, 2, 3, 4, 5)


# Clearing the tuple by creating a new empty tuple
my_tuple = ()
```

```
# Print the modified tuple
print("Cleared tuple:", my_tuple)
```

OUTPUT

```
Cleared tuple: ()
```

EXPLANATION

- ≡ In this example, my_tuple = () creates a new empty tuple.
- ≡ Eeffectively "clearing" the original tuple.

- ✓ Keep in mind that this creates a new tuple object.
- ✓ And any references to the original tuple will still point to the original data unless reassigned.

DICTIONARY ← REMOVING ELEMENTS

- ≡ To remove key-value pairs from a Python dictionary.

You can do it in 3 ways.

USING del KEYWORD:

EXAMPLE

Using the del keyword to delete a specific key-value pair.

```
# Create a dictionary
my_dict = {'a': 1, 'b': 2, 'c': 3}
```

```
# Using 'del' keyword to remove a specific key-value pair
del my_dict['b']
print(my_dict)
```

OUTPUT

```
{'a': 1, 'c': 3}
```

USING pop() KEYWORD:

EXAMPLE

Using the pop() method to remove a specific key-value pair and return its value.

```
# Create a dictionary
my_dict = {'a': 1, 'c': 3}

# Using 'pop()' method to remove a specific key-value pair
value_of_c = my_dict.pop('c')

print(my_dict)
print(value_of_c)
```

OUTPUT

```
{'a': 1}

3
```

USING popitem() KEYWORD:

EXAMPLE

Using the popitem() method to remove and return the last inserted key-value pair.

```
# Create a dictionary
my_dict = {'a': 1}


# Using 'popitem()' method to remove and return the last
inserted key-value pair
last_pair_removed = my_dict.popitem()


print(my_dict)
print(last_pair_removed)
```

OUTPUT

```
{}

('a', 1)
```

SET ← REMOVING ELEMENTS

 ≡ To remove elements to a Python set, you can use remove() methods.

Here's how you can remove elements to a set using remove() methods.

EXAMPLE

```
# Define a set
my_set = {1, 2, 3, 4}


# Removing a single element to the set
my_set.remove(3)


# Print the modified removed set
print(my_set)
```

OUTPUT

```
{1, 2, 4}
```

EXPLANATION

- ≡ In example, we first define a set (my_set).
- ≡ Then, we use the method remove() to remove elements to the set.
- ≡ Finally, we print the modified my_set to verify the changes.
- ✓ Here methods provide flexible ways to remove elements to a set in Python.
- ✓ Allowing you to easily extend the set with new data as needed.

CHAPTER 12

SORT (SORTING) , REVERSE (REVERSING)

IN

DATA STRUCTURES

LIST , TUPLE , DICTIONARY , SET

LIST ← SORT ELEMENTS PERMANENTLY

- ≡ To sort a Python list permanently using the sort() method, you can simply call the sort() method on the list.
- ≡ The sort() method sorts the elements of the list in ascending order by default.

Here's how you can use the sort() method to sort a list permanently.

EXAMPLE

```python
# Define a list
my_list = [3, 1, 4, 1, 5, 9, 2, 6, 5, 3]


# Sort the list permanently
my_list.sort()
```

```
# Print the sorted list
print("Sorted list:", my_list)
```

OUTPUT

```
Sorted list: [1, 1, 2, 3, 3, 4, 5, 5, 6, 9]
```

EXPLANATION

- ≡ We define a list my_list containing unsorted elements.
- ≡ We call the sort() method on the list my_list to sort its elements permanently.
- ≡ The sort() method modifies the original list by sorting its elements in ascending order.
- ≡ We print the sorted list to verify the changes.
- ✓ The sort() method sorts the list in place and does not return a new list.
- ✓ Therefore, the original list is modified directly.

If you want to sort the list in descending order, you can use the reverse=True parameter.

EXAMPLE

```
# Define a list
my_list = [3, 1, 4, 1, 5, 9, 2, 6, 5, 3]
# Sort the list permanently in descending order
my_list.sort(reverse=True)
```

```
# Print the sorted list in descending order
print("Sorted list (descending):", my_list)
```

OUTPUT

```
Sorted list (descending): [9, 6, 5, 5, 4, 3, 3, 2, 1, 1]
```

This will sort the list in descending order instead of ascending order.

LIST ← SORT ELEMENTS TEMPORARILY

- ≡ To sort a Python list temporarily without modifying the original list, you can use the sorted() function.
- ≡ The sorted() function returns a new sorted list based on the elements of the original list.

Here's how you can use the sorted() function to sort a list temporarily:

EXAMPLE

```
# Define a list
my_list = [3, 1, 4, 1, 5, 9, 2, 6, 5, 3]

# Sort the list temporarily
sorted_list = sorted(my_list)
# Print the sorted list
print("Sorted list:", sorted_list)
```

```
# Print the original list to verify that it remains unchanged
print("Original list:", my_list)
```

OUTPUT

```
Sorted list: [1, 1, 2, 3, 3, 4, 5, 5, 6, 9]

Original list: [3, 1, 4, 1, 5, 9, 2, 6, 5, 3]
```

EXPLANATION

- ≡ We define a list my_list containing unsorted elements.
- ≡ We use the sorted() function to sort the elements of my_list temporarily and store the sorted list in a new variable sorted_list.
- ≡ The sorted() function returns a new list containing the sorted elements, leaving the original list my_list unchanged.
- ≡ We print the sorted list to verify the changes, as well as the original list to confirm that it remains unchanged.

- ✓ Unlike the sort() method, which sorts the list in place and modifies the original list, the sorted() function returns a new sorted list without modifying the original list.
- ✓ Therefore, the original list remains unchanged after sorting.

LIST ← REVERSE ELEMENTS

≡ To reverse a list in Python, you can use reverse() method.

Here's how you can reverse a list using reverse() method.

EXAMPLE

≡ The reverse() method reverses the elements of a list in place, modifying the original list.

```python
# Define a list
my_list = [1, 2, 3, 4, 5]

# Reverse the list in place
my_list.reverse()

# Print the reversed list
print("Reversed list:", my_list)
```

OUTPUT

```
Reversed list: [5, 4, 3, 2, 1]
```

TUPLE ← SORT ELEMENTS

≡ To sort a Python tuple permanently using the sorted() method, you can simply call the sorted() method on the tuple.

≡ The sorted() method sorts the elements of the tuple in ascending order by default.

Here's how you can use the sorted() method to sort a tuple permanently.

EXAMPLE

```
# Define a tuple
my_tuple = (2, 5, 3, 1, 4)

# Sort the tuple permanently
my_new_tuple = sorted(my_tuple)

# Print the Newly Created Sorted tuple
print("Newly Created Sorted tuple:", my_new_tuple)
```

OUTPUT

```
Newly Created Sorted tuple: [1, 2, 3, 4, 5]
```

EXPLANATION

≡ We define a tuple my_tuple containing unsorted elements.

- ≡ We call the sorted() method on the tuple my_tuple to sort its elements permanently.
- ≡ The sorted() method modifies the original tuple by sorting its elements in ascending order.
- ≡ We print the sorted tuple to verify the changes.

TUPLE ← REVERSE ELEMENTS

- ≡ To reverse a tuple in Python, you can use reversed() method.

Here's how you can reverse a tuple using reversed() method.

EXAMPLE

The reversed() method reverses the elements of a tuple in place, modifying the original tuple.

```
# Define a tuple
my_tuple = (1, 2, 3, 4, 5)


# Reverse the tuple in place
my_tuple = tuple(reversed(my_tuple))


# Print the reversed tuple
print("Newly Created Reversed tuple:", my_tuple)
```

OUTPUT

```
Newly Created Reversed tuple: (5, 4, 3, 2, 1)
```

DICTIONARY ← SORT ELEMENTS

- ≡ To sort a Python dictionary permanently using the sorted() method, you can simply call the sorted() method on the dictionary.
- ≡ The sorted() method sorts the elements of the dictionary in ascending order by default.

Here's how you can use the sorted() method to sort a dictionary permanently.

EXAMPLE

```python
# Define a dictionary
my_dict = {'a': 1, 'c': 3, 'b': 2}

# Sort the dictionary permanently
my_new_dict = sorted(my_dict)

# Print the Newly Created Sorted dictionary
print("Newly Created Sorted dictionary:", my_new_dict)
```

OUTPUT

```
Newly Created Sorted dictionary: ['a', 'b', 'c']
```

EXPLANATION

- ≡ We define a dictionary my_dict containing unsorted elements.

- ≡ We call the sorted() method on the dictionary my_tuple to sort its elements permanently.
- ≡ The sorted() method modifies the original dictionary by sorting its elements in ascending order.
- ≡ We print the sorted dictionary to verify the changes.

DICTIONARY ← REVERSE ELEMENTS

- ≡ To reverse a tuple in Python, you can use for loop and reversed() method.

Here's how you can reverse a tuple using for loop and reversed() method.

EXAMPLE

- ≡ First, you will initialize a new empty dictionary.
- ≡ For storing the reversed items of the original dictionary.

- ✓ Second, we will use for loop to traverse through the original list.
- ✓ And store every key-value pair in the new empty dictionary after reversing it using reversed() method.

```
# First, Define a Original Dictionary
my_dict1 = {'a': 1, 'c': 3, 'b': 2}
print("Printing Original Dictionary ", my_dict1)


# Define a Empty Dictionary
# For storing the reversed items of the original dictionary.
```

```
my_dict2 = {}

# Second, we will use for loop to traverse through the original
   list.
for key in reversed(my_dict1):

# And store every key-value pair in the new empty dictionary
   after reversing it using reversed() method.
   my_dict2[key] = my_dict1[key]

print("Newly Created Reversed dictionary:", my_dict2)
```

OUTPUT

```
Printing Original Dictionary  {'a': 1, 'c': 3, 'b': 2}
Newly Created Reversed dictionary: {'b': 2, 'c': 3, 'a': 1}
```

SET ← SORT ELEMENTS

- ≡ To sort a Python set permanently using the sorted() method, you can simply call the sorted() method on the set.
- ≡ The sorted() method sorts the elements of the set in ascending order by default.

Here's how you can use the sorted() method to sort a set permanently.

EXAMPLE

```
# Define a set
my_set = {4, 1, 5, 2, 3}

# Sort the set permanently
my_new_set = sorted(my_set)

# Print the Newly Created Sorted dictionary
print("Newly Created Sorted set:", my_new_set)
```

OUTPUT

```
Newly Created Sorted set: [1, 2, 3, 4, 5]
```

EXPLANATION

- ≡ We define a set my_set containing unsorted elements.
- ≡ We call the sorted() method on the set my_set to sort its elements permanently.
- ≡ The sorted() method modifies the original set by sorting its elements in ascending order.
- ≡ We print the sorted set to verify the changes.

CHAPTER 13

LOOPS (LOOPING)

IN

DATA STRUCTURES

LIST , TUPLE , DICTIONARY , SET

LIST ← LOOP ELEMENTS

≡ You can loop through the entire contents of a Python list using a variety of methods, including using a for loop, a while loop, or iterating over the list with a comprehension.

≡ The most common and straightforward approach is to use a for loop.

Here's how you can do it.

EXAMPLE

Using for loop.

```python
# Define a list
my_list = [1, 2, 3, 4, 5]


# Loop through the entire list using a for loop
for item in my_list:
```

```
    print(item)
```

OUTPUT

```
1

2

3

4

5
```

EXPLANATION

- ≡ We define a list my_list containing five elements.
- ≡ We use a for loop to iterate over each element (item) in the list.
- ≡ Inside the loop, we print each element (item).

- ✓ This loop iterates through the entire list, executing the code block inside the loop once for each element in the list.

EXAMPLE

Using while loop.

```
# Define a list
my_list = [1, 2, 3, 4, 5]


# Loop through the entire list using a while loop
index = 0
```

```
while index < len(my_list):
    print(my_list[index])
    index += 1
```

OUTPUT

```
1
2
3
4
5
```

TUPLE ← LOOP ELEMENTS

- ≡ You can loop through the entire contents of a Python tuple using a variety of methods, including using a for loop, a while loop, or iterating over the tuple with a comprehension.
- ≡ The most common and straightforward approach is to use a for loop.

Here's how you can do it.

EXAMPLE

Using for loop.

```
# Define a tuple
my_tuple = (1, 2, 3, 4, 5)
```

```
# Loop through all values in the tuple using a for loop
for value in my_tuple:
    print(value)
```

OUTPUT

```
1
2
3
4
5
```

EXPLANATION

- ≡ We define a tuple my_tuple containing five elements.
- ≡ We use a for loop to iterate over each element (value) in the tuple.
- ≡ Inside the loop, we print each element (value).

- ✓ This loop iterates through the entire tuple, executing the code block inside the loop once for each element in the tuple.

DICTIONARY ← LOOP ELEMENTS

- ≡ You can loop through all key-value pairs in a Python dictionary using a for loop.
- ≡ Python dictionaries provide several methods to access keys, values, or both.

Here's how you can loop through all key-value pairs in a dictionary.

EXAMPLE

```python
my_dict = {'name': 'John', 'age': 30, 'city': 'New York'}


# Loop through all key-value pairs
for key, value in my_dict.items():
    print(key, '=', value)
```

OUTPUT

```
name = John
age = 30
city = New York
```

EXPLANATION

- ≡ In this example, my_dict.items() returns a view object that provides a dynamic view of the dictionary's key-value pairs.

- ≡ The for loop iterates over each key-value pair, and key and value are assigned to each key-value pair respectively.
- ≡ Inside the loop, you can access both the key and value of each pair and perform any desired operations.

  ✓ Using .items() is the most common and efficient way to loop through all key-value pairs in a dictionary in Python.

DICTIONARY ← LOOP KEYS

USING keys METHOD:

EXAMPLE

You can loop through all the keys in a Python dictionary using a for loop.

```
# Create a dictionary
my_dict = {'a': 1, 'b': 2, 'c': 3}


# Loop through all the keys
for key in my_dict:
    print(key)
```

OUTPUT

```
a
b
c
```

EXPLANATION

In this loop, key iterates over each key in the dictionary my_dict, allowing you to perform operations using each key.

DICTIONARY ← LOOP VALUES

Using values() method:

EXAMPLE

You can loop through all the values in a Python dictionary using the values() method or directly iterating over the dictionary.

```python
# Create a dictionary
my_dict = {'a': 1, 'b': 2, 'c': 3}

# Loop through all the values using values() method
for value in my_dict.values():
    print(value)
```

OUTPUT

```
1
2
3
```

EXPLANATION

≡ It allow you to iterate through all the values in the dictionary, giving you access to each value one by one.

SET ← LOOP ELEMENTS

≡ You can access set items is by traversing the set using a loop , such as a for loop.

≡ By iterating over the set, you can access each element one by one and perform operations on them as needed.

≡ In Python, sets are unordered collections of unique elements.

≡ Sets do not have a positional index for their elements.

≡ This means that you cannot access individual elements of a set directly by specifying an index.

EXAMPLE

```python
# Define a set
my_set = {1, 2, 3, 4}


# Accessing element of the set
for my_set1 in my_set:


# Print the elements of set
print(my_set1)
```

OUTPUT

```
1
2
3
```

EXPLANATION

- ≡ In example, we first define a set (my_set).
- ≡ Then, we will traverse the set using a loop , such as a for loop.
- ≡ By iterating over the set, we will access each element one by one of the set.
- ≡ Finally, we print the elements of my_set to one by one.

CHAPTER 14

SLICE (SLICING) , SHUFFLE (SHUFFLING)

IN

DATA STRUCTURES

LIST , TUPLE , DICTIONARY , SET

LIST ← SLICE ELEMENTS

- ≡ In Python, slicing a list allows you to extract a portion of the list based on specified start and end indices.

The basic syntax for slicing a list is.

SYNTAX

```
my_list[start_index:end_index]
```

- ≡ Here, start_index is the index where the slice starts, and end_index is the index where the slice ends.
- ≡ If start_index is omitted, slicing starts from the beginning of the list.
- ≡ If end_index is omitted, slicing continues to the end of the list.

Here are a few examples of list slicing.

EXAMPLE

Slicing from the beginning to a specific index.

```
my_list = ['apple', 'banana', 'cherry', 'date', 'elderberry']


# Slice from index 0 to index 3
slice_result = my_list[:3]


print(slice_result)
```

OUTPUT

```
['apple', 'banana', 'cherry']
```

EXAMPLE

Slicing from a specific index to the end.

```
my_list = ['apple', 'banana', 'cherry', 'date', 'elderberry']


# Slice from index 2 to the end
slice_result = my_list[2:]


print(slice_result)
```

OUTPUT

```
['cherry', 'date', 'elderberry']
```

EXAMPLE

Slicing with both start and end indices.

```
my_list = ['apple', 'banana', 'cherry', 'date', 'elderberry']

# Slice from index 1 to index 4
slice_result = my_list[1:4]

print(slice_result)
```

OUTPUT

```
['banana', 'cherry', 'date']
```

EXAMPLE

Slicing with negative indices.

```
my_list = ['apple', 'banana', 'cherry', 'date', 'elderberry']

# Slice from the third-to-last element to the last element
slice_result = my_list[-3:-1]

print(slice_result)
```

OUTPUT

['cherry', 'date']

- ✓ Remember that when slicing a list, the original list remains unchanged, and a new list containing the sliced elements is created.
- ✓ If you omit both start_index and end_index, the slice will contain all elements of the list, effectively creating a shallow copy of the original list.

LIST ← SHUFFLE ELEMENTS

≡ To shuffle a list or sequence in Python, you can use the
≡ random. shuffle() function from the random module.

Here's how you can do it.

EXAMPLE

```
import random

my_list = [1, 2, 3, 4, 5]

# Shuffle the list
random.shuffle(my_list)

print("Shuffled list:", my_list)
```

OUTPUT

```
Shuffled list: [1, 2, 3, 4, 5]   Pending
```

TUPLE ← SLICE ELEMENTS

≡ Accessing elements of a tuple in Python is similar to
   accessing elements of other sequences like lists.
≡ You can use indexing to access individual elements or
   slicing to access multiple elements.

Here's how you can do it.

EXAMPLE

```
# Define a tuple
my_tuple = (1, 2, 3, 4, 5)


# Accessing multiple elements using slicing
# Elements from index 1 to index 3 (exclusive)
slice_of_tuple = my_tuple[1:4]


# Elements from index 1 to index 3 (exclusive)
print("Slice of tuple:", slice_of_tuple)
```

OUTPUT

```
Slice of tuple: (2, 3, 4)
```

EXPLANATION

- ≡ We define a list my_tuple containing five elements.
- ≡ We use square brackets [] to access elements by their index within the tuple.
- ≡ Positive indices refer to elements starting from the beginning of the tuple, while negative indices refer to elements starting from the end of the tuple.
- ≡ We print the values of the elements at index 1, 2, 3 to demonstrate accessing elements by index.

DICTIONARY ← SLICE ELEMENTS

≡ If you want to slice dictionary elements means printing its elements in a sorter form.

You want to create a smaller, new, dictionary.

First , convert dictionary into a list and slice the list elements.

Second , convert list back to a dictionary elements.

EXAMPLE

```python
# Define a Dictionary
my_dict = {'a': 1, 'c': 3, 'b': 2, 'e': 5, 'd': 4}

# Printing Original dictionary
print("Printing Original dictionary:")
print(my_dict)

# Convert dictionary into a list
my_dict_list = list(my_dict.items())

# Printing Converted dictionary into a list
print("Printing Converted dictionary into a list:")
print(my_dict_list)

# Printing sliced elements of list
sliced_dict_list = my_dict_list[1:4]
```

```
# Printing sliced elements of list
print("Printing sliced elements of list:")
print(sliced_dict_list)

# Printing sliced elements of dictionary
print("Printing sliced elements of dictionary:")
print(dict(sliced_dict_list))
```

OUTPUT

```
Printing Original dictionary:
{'a': 1, 'c': 3, 'b': 2, 'e': 5, 'd': 4}

Printing Converted dictionary into a list:
[('a', 1), ('c', 3), ('b', 2), ('e', 5), ('d', 4)]

Printing sliced elements of list:
[('c', 3), ('b', 2), ('e', 5)]

Printing sliced elements of dictionary:
{'c': 3, 'b': 2, 'e': 5}
```

DICTIONARY ← SHUFFLE ELEMENTS

≡ If you want to shuffle elements means printing its elements in a different, non-default, order.

First, convert dictionary into a list and re-arrange the list elements.

Here's how you can do it.

EXAMPLE

```
import random


# Define a Dictionary
my_dict = {'a': 1, 'c': 3, 'b': 2}


# Printing Original dictionary
print("Printing Original dictionary:")
print(my_dict)


# Convert dictionary into a list
base = list(my_dict.keys())


# Printing Converted dictionary into a list
print("Printing Converted dictionary into a list:")
print([(b, my_dict[b]) for b in base])
```

```
# Suffling or re-arranging the elements of list
random.shuffle(base)


# Printing Suffling or re-arranging the elements of list
print("Printing Suffling or re-arranging the elements of list:")
print([(b, my_dict[b]) for b in base])
```

OUTPUT

```
Printing Original dictionary:
{'a': 1, 'c': 3, 'b': 2}

Printing Converted dictionary into a list:
[('a', 1), ('c', 3), ('b', 2)]

Printing Suffling or re-arranging the elements of list:
[('b', 2), ('c', 3), ('a', 1)]
```

CHAPTER 15

OBJECT ORIENTED PROGRAMMING

IN PYTHON

MODULES

INTRODUCTION , CREATE , IMPORT SYNTAX

MODULES ← INTRODUCTION

- ≡ A Python module is a file containing Python code.
- ≡ Which can define functions, classes, and variables.
- ≡ The purpose of a Python module is to organize related code into a reusable and shareable unit.

- ✓ Modules provide a way to structure large Python projects into smaller, manageable components.
- ✓ Making it easier to maintain, test, and collaborate on code.

MODULES ← PURPOSE , BENEFITS

CODE ORGANIZATION:

- ≡ Modules help organize code by grouping related functionality together.
- ≡ This makes it easier to understand and maintain the codebase.

ENCAPSULATION:

- ≡ Modules provide a way to encapsulate code into separate namespaces.
- ≡ This helps prevent naming conflicts and allows you to use the same names for variables and functions.
- ≡ In different modules without causing conflicts.

REUSABILITY:

- ≡ Modules can be reused in multiple projects or within the same project.
- ≡ Once defined, a module can be imported into other Python scripts or modules.
- ≡ Allowing you to reuse code without duplication.

ABSTRACTION:

- ≡ Modules allow you to abstract away implementation details and expose only the necessary interfaces to users.
- ≡ This promotes a clean and modular design.
- ≡ Where each module can be treated as a black box with well-defined inputs and outputs.

SCOPING:

- ≡ Modules define their own scope.
- ≡ Which helps avoid polluting the global namespace.
- ≡ Variables and functions defined within a module are accessible only within that module unless explicitly imported or exported.

NAMESPACING:

- ≡ Modules provide a way to organize and manage namespaces in Python.
- ≡ Each module has its own namespace.
- ≡ Which helps avoid naming conflicts and provides a clean separation of concerns.

- ✓ Python modules play a crucial role in structuring and organizing Python code, promoting modularity, reusability, and maintainability.
- ✓ They enable developers to build complex applications by breaking them down into smaller, more manageable components.

MODULES ← CREATE

- ≡ To create a Python module, you simply need to create a Python file (.py).
- ≡ Containing the code you want to include in the module.

Here's a step-by-step guide on how to create a Python module.

CREATE A PYTHON FILE:

- ≡ Create a new file with a .py extension.
- ≡ This file will contain the code for your module.
- ≡ For example, you can name it mymodule.py.

WRITE MODULE CODE:

- ≡ Write the Python code for your module in the created file.
- ≡ This can include function definitions, class definitions, variable assignments, and any other Python code you want to include in the module.

DEFINE MODULE INTERFACE:

- ≡ Decide which functions, classes, and variables you want to make accessible to users of your module.
- ≡ These will be the public interface of your module.

SAVE THE FILE:

Save the Python file containing your module code.

USE THE MODULE:

You can now import and use your module in other Python scripts or modules by using the import statement.

EXAMPLE

Here's a simple Python module named mymodule.py .

```
# mymodule.py


def greet(name):
    return f"Hello, {name}!"


def add(a, b):
    return a + b


PI = 3.14159
```

To use this module in another Python script, you would import it like this.

```
# main.py

import mymodule

print(mymodule.greet("Alice"))
```

```
print(mymodule.add(2, 3))
print(mymodule.PI)
```

OUTPUT

```
Hello, Alice!
5
3.14159
```

MODULES ← FILE , FOLDER STRUCTURE CONVENTION

≡ As for the file/folder structure convention for a Python module.
  It's common practice to organize related modules into packages.
≡ A package is a directory that contains one or more Python modules and an __init__.py file.

my_package/

    ≡ __init__.py
    ≡ module1.py
    ≡ module2.py
    ≡ subpackage/

        ≡ __init__.py
        ≡ submodule1.py
        ≡ submodule2.py

EXPLANATION

- ≡ my_package is the top-level package directory.
- ≡ __init__.py files indicate that the directories are Python packages and can contain module code.
- ≡ module1.py and module2.py are Python modules directly within the my_package package.
- ≡ subpackage is a subpackage directory within the my_package package.
- ≡ submodule1.py and submodule2.py are Python modules within the subpackage subpackage.

- ✓ This structure allows you to organize your modules into logical groups and namespaces, making it easier to manage and maintain larger codebases.

MODULES ← IMPORT SYNTAX

- ≡ In Python, the import statement is used to include various Python modules into your code.
- ✓ There are several syntaxes you can use depending on what you want to achieve.

MODULES ← IMPORT ENTIRE MODULE

SYNTAX

```
import module_name
```

EXAMPLE

```
import math
```

MODULES ← IMPORT WITH ALIAS

SYNTAX

```
import module_name as alias
```

EXAMPLE

```
import numpy as np
```

MODULES : ATTRIBUTES , FUNCTION

MODULES ←IMPORT SPECIFIC ATTRIBUTES FROM A MODULE

SYNTAX

```
from module_name import attribute_name1, attribute_name2,
...
```

EXAMPLE

```
from math import sqrt, pi
```

MODULES ← IMPORT ALL ATTRIBUTES FROM A MODULE

SYNTAX

```
from module_name import *
```

- ≡ This imports all attributes defined in the module.
- ≡ But it's generally discouraged because it can lead to namespace pollution.
- ≡ And make it unclear where certain functions or classes come from.

EXAMPLE

```
from math import *
```

MODULES ← IMPORT SUB MODULE

SYNTAX

```
import package_name.module_name
```

EXAMPLE

```
import matplotlib.pyplot as plt
```

- ✓ These are the primary ways to use the import statement in Python.
- ✓ Each has its use case depending on the requirements of your program and your coding style preferences.

Modules ← Import All Function

- ≡ To import all functions and attributes from a module in Python, you can use the * wildcard character with the import statement.
- ≡ However, it's generally discouraged because it can lead to namespace pollution and make it unclear where certain functions or classes come from.

SYNTAX

```
from module_name import *
```

Replace module_name with the name of the module you want to import from.

EXAMPLE

```
from math import *
```

EXPLANATION

- ≡ This imports all functions and attributes from the math module into the current namespace.
- ≡ However, it's recommended to import only the specific functions or attributes you need from a module to keep your code clean and avoid potential naming conflicts.

MODULES : IMPORT AS ALIAS

MODULES ← IMPORT AS ALIAS
← ALIAS FOR A MODULE

SYNTAX

```
import module_name as alias
```

EXAMPLE

```
import numpy as np
```

EXPLANATION

≡ In the above examples, np is an alias for the numpy module.

In the above examples, np is an alias for the numpy module.

MODULES ← IMPORT AS ALIAS
← ALIAS FOR A FUNCTION OR CLASS

SYNTAX

```
from module_name import
                    function_name_or_class_name as alias
```

EXAMPLE

```
from math import sqrt as square_root
```

EXPLANATION

≡ In the above examples, square_root is an alias for the sqrt function from the math module.

MODULES : FUNCTIONS , CLASSES

MODULES ← IMPORT SPECIFIC FUNCTION

- ≡ You can import specific Python functions using the import statement along with the from keyword.

SYNTAX

```
from module_name import function_name1, function_name2,...
```

Replace module_name with the name of the module containing the functions you want to import, and list the function names you want to import separated by commas.

Let's say you want to import the sqrt and cos functions from the math module. **EXAMPLE**

```
from math import sqrt, cos
print(sqrt(4))
print(cos(0))
```

Now you can use these functions directly in your code without prefixing them with the module name. **OUTPUT**

```
2.0
1.0
```

EXPLANATION

- ≡ This syntax is useful when you only need specific functions from a module and don't want to import the entire module.
- ≡ It can also make your code more readable by clearly indicating which functions are being used.

MODULES ← IMPORT CLASSES

To import classes from a module in Python, you can use the import statement along with the from keyword, similar to how you import functions.

SYNTAX

```
from module_name import ClassName1, ClassName2, ...
```

Replace module_name with the name of the module containing the classes you want to import, and list the class names you want to import separated by commas.

Let's say you have a module named my_module containing two classes Dog and Cat, and you want to import both classes.

EXAMPLE

```
from my_module import Dog, Cat


# Now you can create objects of these classes directly in your code.

my_dog = Dog("Buddy")

my_cat = Cat("Whiskers")
```

EXPLANATION

- ≡ This syntax is useful when you only need specific classes from a module and don't want to import the entire module.
- ≡ It can also make your code more readable by clearly indicating which classes are being used.

CHAPTER 16

OBJECT ORIENTED PROGRAMMING

IN PYTHON

CLASS , INHERITANCE , ABSTRACT CLASS

INTRODUCTION , CREATE , IMPORT SYNTAX

CLASS

CLASS ← INTRODUCTION

- ≡ In Python, a class is a blueprint for creating objects (instances).
- ≡ It defines the properties (attributes) and behaviors (methods) that all objects created from it will have.

- ✓ Classes are fundamental to object-oriented programming (OOP).
- ✓ A programming paradigm that models real-world entities as objects with attributes and behaviors.

CLASS ← KEY CONCEPTS

ATTRIBUTES:

≡ These are variables that store data associated with the class or its instances.

METHODS:

≡ These are functions defined within a class that can perform operations on the class's data.

INSTANCES:

≡ These are individual objects created from a class.
≡ Each instance has its own set of attributes and can call the class's methods.

INHERITANCE:

≡ This is a feature of OOP that allows a class (called a subclass or derived class) to inherit attributes and methods from another class (called a superclass or base class).
≡ It promotes code reusability and allows for creating specialized classes based on existing ones.

CLASS ← USING CLASSES IN DIFFERENT SCENARIO

ENCAPSULATION:

≡ Classes allow you to encapsulate data and functionality together.
≡ This means that data and the operations that manipulate it are bundled together within the class, promoting modularity and making the code easier to understand and maintain.

ABSTRACTION:

- ≡ Classes provide a way to model real-world entities with their attributes and behaviors.
- ≡ They abstract away the details of implementation and allow you to work with higher-level concepts.

CODE REUSABILITY:

- ≡ By defining classes and using inheritance, you can reuse code across different parts of your program.
- ≡ This promotes code organization, reduces redundancy, and makes it easier to manage complex systems.

POLYMORPHISM:

- ≡ Classes support polymorphism, which allows different objects to be treated as instances of the same class, even if they are of different types.
- ≡ This promotes flexibility and makes it easier to work with heterogeneous collections of objects.
- ✓ In summary, Python classes are essential for building modular, maintainable, and scalable software.
- ✓ They provide a way to structure code, encapsulate data and behavior, promote code reuse, and model real-world entities in a flexible and understandable manner.

CLASS : CREATING NEW INSTANCE

__init__() ← CREATING NEW INSTANCE OF CLASS

- ≡ In Python, __init__() is a special method (also known as a constructor) that is automatically called when a new instance of a class is created.
- ≡ It is used to initialize the attributes of the newly created object.

- ✓ The __init__() method is optional.
- ✓ But it is commonly used to set up the initial state of an object.

SYNTAX

```
class ClassName:
    def __init__(self, parameter1, parameter2, ...):
        # Initialization code here
```

EXPLANATION

- ≡ self: The first parameter of the __init__() method is always self, which refers to the current instance of the class.
- ≡ It is used to access the attributes and methods of the instance within the class.
- ≡ parameter1, parameter2, ...: These are the parameters that you want to pass when creating an instance of the class.
- ≡ You can define any number of parameters here, depending on the initialization requirements of your class.

EXAMPLE

```python
class Person:
    def __init__(self, name, age):
        self.name = name
        self.age = age


# Creating instances of the Person class
person1 = Person("Alice", 30)
person2 = Person("Bob", 25)


# Accessing attributes of the instances
print(person1.name)
print(person1.age)

print(person2.name)
print(person2.age)
```

OUTPUT

```
Alice
30

Bob
25
```

EXPLANATION

- In this example, the __init__() method initializes the name and age attributes of each Person object when it is created.
- When you create a new Person object (person1 and person2), you provide values for name and age, which are then assigned to the corresponding attributes of the object.

__init__() ← CREATING NEW INSTANCE OF CLASS
← STEP BY STEP

STEP 1:

DEFINE THE CLASS:

- Define the blueprint for the objects you want to create by writing a class definition.

STEP 2:

INSTANTIATE THE CLASS:

- Use the class name followed by parentheses () to create an instance of the class.

EXAMPLE

```
# Define the class
class MyClass:
    def __init__(self, parameter1, parameter2):
        self.parameter1 = parameter1
```

```
        self.parameter2 = parameter2

# Instantiate the class
my_instance = MyClass(value1, value2)

# Using my_instance to access the attributes and methods of
    the MyClass object
print(my_instance.parameter1)
print(my_instance.parameter2)
```

OUTPUT

```
value1
value2
```

EXPLANATION

≡ We define a class named MyClass.
≡ Inside the class, there is an __init__() method that
  initializes the instance attributes (parameter1 and
  parameter2) with the values passed as arguments.

≡ We then create an instance of MyClass by calling
  MyClass(value1, value2).
≡ This invokes the __init__() method with the specified
  values for parameter1 and parameter2, creating a new
  instance of the class.

- ≡ The newly created instance is assigned to the variable my_instance.
- ≡ Now, you can use my_instance to access the attributes and methods of the MyClass object.

- ✓ Replace value1 and value2 with the values you want to initialize the instance with.
- ✓ This is how you make an instance from a Python class.

CLASS : ATTRIBUTES , METHOD

CLASS ← ACCESSING ATTRIBUTES USING A CLASS

≡ To access an attribute from a Python class, you use dot notation (.) followed by the attribute name.

STEP 1:

≡ First, you need to create an instance of the class.

STEP 2:

≡ Then, you can use dot notation to access the attributes of that instance.

EXAMPLE

```
class MyClass:
    def __init__(self, attribute):
        self.attribute = attribute

# Create an instance of MyClass
my_instance = MyClass("value")

# Access the attribute using dot notation
print(my_instance.attribute)
```

EXPLANATION

- ≡ We define a class named MyClass with an __init__() method that initializes an attribute (self.attribute) with the value passed as an argument.
- ≡ We create an instance of MyClass called my_instance and pass the value "value" to the constructor.
- ≡ We then use dot notation (my_instance.attribute) to access the value of the attribute attribute of the my_instance object.

- ✓ This will print "value", which is the value assigned to the attribute attribute of the my_instance object.

CLASS ← CALLING A METHOD USING A CLASS

STEP 1:

- ≡ Create an instance of the class.

STEP 2:

- ≡ Use dot notation (.) followed by the method name to call the method on that instance.

EXAMPLE

```
class MyClass:
   def __init__(self, attribute):
      self.attribute = attribute


   def my_method(self):
```

```
    print("Hello from my_method!")

# Create an instance of MyClass
my_instance = MyClass("value")


# Call the method using dot notation
my_instance.my_method()
```

OUTPUT

```
"Hello from my_method!"
```

EXPLANATION

- ≡ We define a class named MyClass with an __init__()
  method that initializes an attribute (self.attribute) with the
  value passed as an argument, and a my_method() method.
- ≡ We create an instance of MyClass called my_instance and
  pass the value "value" to the constructor.
- ≡ We then call the my_method() method on the my_instance
  object using dot notation (my_instance.my_method()).

- ✓ This will print "Hello from my_method!", indicating that
  the method has been called successfully on the instance of
  the class.

INHERITANCE

INHERITANCE ← INTRODUCTION

- ≡ Class inheritance in Python allows a class (subclass) to inherit attributes and methods from another class (superclass).
- ≡ This means that the subclass can access and use the attributes and methods of the superclass without redefining them.

- ≡ Inheritance creates a parent-child relationship between classes, where the subclass inherits the characteristics of the superclass and can also have its own additional attributes and methods.

SYNTAX

```
class Superclass:
    # Attributes and methods

class Subclass(Superclass):
    # Additional attributes and methods
```

EXPLANATION

- ≡ Subclass is the subclass that inherits from Superclass.
- ≡ Subclass can access all attributes and methods of Superclass and can also define its own additional attributes and methods.

INHERITANCE ← WHEN , WHY , NEED OF INHERITANCE

CODE REUSABILITY:

≡ Inheritance allows you to reuse code by defining common attributes and methods in a superclass.

≡ Subclasses can then inherit these common characteristics without having to redefine them, reducing code duplication.

MODULARITY AND EXTENSIBILITY:

≡ Inheritance promotes modularity by organizing code into logical hierarchies.

≡ Subclasses can extend the functionality of the superclass by adding new methods or overriding existing ones, thus providing flexibility and extensibility to the codebase.

ABSTRACTION AND ENCAPSULATION:

≡ Inheritance helps in creating abstract classes that define a common interface or behavior for a group of related classes.

≡ It allows you to encapsulate common functionality in the superclass, making the code more manageable and understandable.

POLYMORPHISM:

≡ Inheritance facilitates polymorphism, which allows objects of different classes to be treated uniformly based on their common superclass.

≡ This enables you to write code that operates on objects of the superclass type but can also handle objects of the subclass type, providing flexibility and code reuse.

SPECIALIZATION:

≡ Subclasses can specialize or customize the behavior of the superclass by adding new functionality or modifying existing functionality.

≡ This allows you to tailor classes to specific requirements while maintaining a consistent interface across related classes.

✓ Overall, inheritance is a powerful mechanism in object-oriented programming that promotes code reuse, modularity, and extensibility, making it easier to manage and maintain complex systems.

✓ However, it should be used judiciously to avoid creating overly complex class hierarchies and tight coupling between classes.

INHERITANCE ← SYNTAX

≡ In Python, creating inheritance between classes involves defining a new class that inherits from an existing class.

SYNTAX

```
class BaseClass:
    # Attributes and methods of the base class
```

```
class DerivedClass(BaseClass):
    # Additional attributes and methods of the derived class
```

EXPLANATION

- BaseClass is the name of the existing class from which you want to inherit.
- DerivedClass is the name of the new class that you're creating, which will inherit from BaseClass.
- DerivedClass is said to be a subclass of BaseClass, and BaseClass is said to be the superclass or parent class of DerivedClass.

- ✓ By inheriting from BaseClass, DerivedClass gains access to all the attributes and methods defined in BaseClass.
- ✓ Additionally, you can define new attributes and methods specific to DerivedClass within its own class definition.

EXAMPLE

```
class Animal:
    def sound(self):
        print("Some generic sound")

# Dog inherits from Animal
class Dog(Animal):
    def sound(self):
        print("Woof")
```

```
# Cat inherits from Animal
class Cat(Animal):
    def sound(self):
        print("Meow")


# Create instances of subclasses
dog = Dog()
cat = Cat()


# Call methods from the superclass and subclasses
dog.sound()
cat.sound()
```

OUTPUT

```
Woof
Meow
```

EXPLANATION

- In this example, Dog and Cat are subclasses of Animal.
- They inherit the sound() method from Animal but provide their own implementation of the method.
- When you call sound() on instances of Dog and Cat, it prints the sound specific to each subclass.

INHERITANCE ← __init__() METHODS

≡ To define and use the __init__() method for a child class (subclass) in Python inheritance, you can override the __init__() method of the parent class (superclass).

≡ This allows you to customize the initialization process for instances of the child class while still leveraging the initialization logic of the parent class if needed.

EXAMPLE

```python
class ParentClass:
    def __init__(self, parent_attribute):
        self.parent_attribute = parent_attribute

        print("ParentClass initialized with:", self.parent_attribute)


class ChildClass(ParentClass):
    def __init__(self, parent_attribute, child_attribute):

        # Call the __init__() method of the parent class
        super().__init__(parent_attribute)
        self.child_attribute = child_attribute

        print("ChildClass initialized with:", self.child_attribute)
```

```
# Create an instance of the child class
child_obj = ChildClass("Parent Data", "Child Data")
```

EXPLANATION

- ParentClass defines an __init__() method that initializes an attribute parent_attribute.
- ChildClass is a subclass of ParentClass and defines its own __init__() method.

- Inside ChildClass's __init__() method, super().__init__(parent_attribute) calls the __init__() method of the parent class (ParentClass) to initialize the parent_attribute.
- After initializing the parent attribute, the __init__() method of ChildClass initializes its own attribute child_attribute.
- When you create an instance of ChildClass, both ParentClass's and ChildClass's __init__() methods are called, in the order defined in the inheritance hierarchy.

✓ This approach ensures that the initialization logic defined in the parent class is executed before the initialization logic of the child class, allowing for proper initialization of attributes in both classes.

INHERITANCE ← ATTRIBUTES AND METHODS

- ≡ In Python, you can define attributes and methods for a child class (subclass) in the same way you define them for any other class.
- ≡ The child class can have its own attributes and methods in addition to those inherited from the parent class (superclass).

EXAMPLE

```python
class ParentClass:
    def __init__(self, parent_attribute):
        self.parent_attribute = parent_attribute

    def parent_method(self):
        print("This is a method from ParentClass")

class ChildClass(ParentClass):
    def __init__(self, parent_attribute, child_attribute):
        super().__init__(parent_attribute)
        self.child_attribute = child_attribute

    def child_method(self):
        print("This is a method from ChildClass")

# Create an instance of the child class
child_obj = ChildClass("Parent Data", "Child Data")
```

```
# Access attributes and call methods of the child class
print("Parent attribute:", child_obj.parent_attribute)
print("Child attribute:", child_obj.child_attribute)


child_obj.parent_method()
child_obj.child_method()
```

EXPLANATION

- ParentClass defines an __init__() method and a method called parent_method().

- ChildClass is a subclass of ParentClass and defines its own __init__() method and a method called child_method().
- Inside ChildClass's __init__() method, it calls the __init__() method of the parent class using super().__init__() to initialize the parent attribute. It also initializes its own attribute.
- ChildClass's child_method() method is specific to the child class and can only be called on instances of ChildClass.
- You can access both parent and child attributes and call methods from both classes on instances of ChildClass.

✓ This demonstrates how you can define attributes and methods for a child class in Python.
✓ The child class inherits attributes and methods from the parent class but can also have its own unique attributes and methods.

INHERITANCE ← OVERRIDING METHODS

- ≡ In Python, you can override methods from the parent class in a child class by defining a method with the same name in the child class.
- ≡ When an instance of the child class calls the method, the overridden method in the child class will be executed instead of the method from the parent class.

EXAMPLE

```python
class ParentClass:
    def some_method(self):
        print("This is a method from ParentClass")


class ChildClass(ParentClass):
    def some_method(self):
        print("This is an overridden method from ChildClass")


# Create an instance of the child class
child_obj = ChildClass()

# Call the overridden method
child_obj.some_method()
```

OUTPUT

```
This is an overridden method from ChildClass
```

EXPLANATION

- ParentClass defines a method called some_method().
- ChildClass is a subclass of ParentClass and defines its own version of the some_method() method.
- When you call some_method() on an instance of ChildClass, it calls the overridden method from ChildClass, not the method from ParentClass.

✓ This demonstrates how you can override methods from the parent class in Python.
✓ Overriding methods allows child classes to provide their own implementations of methods inherited from the parent class, providing flexibility and customization in object-oriented programming.

ABSTRACT BASE CLASS

ABSTRACT BASE CLASS ← INTRODUCTION

- ≡ Abstract Base Classes (ABCs) in Python are classes that cannot be instantiated directly but are meant to be subclassed.
- ≡ They define a set of abstract methods that must be implemented by concrete subclasses.

- ≡ ABCs provide a way to define a common interface or behavior for a group of related classes while enforcing a contract that specifies which methods must be implemented by subclasses.

- ✓ To use Abstract Base Classes in Python, you need to import the abc module from the standard library, which provides the ABC class and other utilities for defining and working with abstract classes.

EXAMPLE

```python
from abc import ABC, abstractmethod


class Shape(ABC):
  @abstractmethod
  def area(self):
    pass
```

```python
    @abstractmethod
    def perimeter(self):
        pass

class Rectangle(Shape):
    def __init__(self, length, width):
        self.length = length
        self.width = width

    def area(self):
        return self.length * self.width

    def perimeter(self):
        return 2 * (self.length + self.width)

# Attempting to instantiate the Shape class directly will raise
an error
# shape = Shape()
# This will raise TypeError: Can't instantiate abstract class
    Shape with abstract methods area, perimeter

# Instantiate a subclass of Shape
rectangle = Rectangle(5, 4)
```

```
print("Area:", rectangle.area())

print("Perimeter:", rectangle.perimeter())
```

OUTPUT

```
Area: 20

Perimeter: 18
```

EXPLANATION

- ≡ Shape is an abstract base class that defines two abstract methods: area() and perimeter().
- ≡ The abstractmethod decorator from the abc module is used to mark these methods as abstract, indicating that they must be implemented by concrete subclasses.

- ≡ Rectangle is a concrete subclass of Shape that implements both area() and perimeter() methods.

- ≡ You cannot instantiate the Shape class directly because it is abstract and contains abstract methods. Attempting to do so will raise a TypeError.
- ≡ You can instantiate Rectangle, which is a concrete subclass of Shape, and use its methods.
- ✓ Abstract Base Classes provide a way to define a common interface or behavior for a group of related classes, ensuring that subclasses implement the required methods.
- ✓ They are useful for enforcing contracts and promoting code clarity and maintainability in object-oriented programming.

ABSTRACT BASE CLASS ← CONCEPT

- ≡ Abstract classes in Python serve as templates for other classes.
- ≡ They are not meant to be instantiated directly but instead are designed to be subclassed.

- ≡ Abstract classes define a blueprint for how subclasses should be structured and what methods they should implement.
- ≡ They typically contain one or more abstract methods, which are methods that are declared but not implemented in the abstract class itself.
- ✓ Subclasses must provide concrete implementations for these abstract methods.

CANNOT INSTANTIATED DIRECTLY:

- ≡ Abstract classes cannot be instantiated directly because they contain one or more abstract methods that are not implemented.
- ✓ Attempting to create an instance of an abstract class will result in an error.

PROVIDE A TEMPLATE FOR SUBCLASSES:

- ≡ Abstract classes provide a blueprint or template for how subclasses should be structured.
- ✓ They define common methods or attributes that subclasses are expected to implement or use.

CONTAIN ONE OR MORE ABSTRACT METHODS:

- ≡ Abstract methods are methods declared in an abstract class but not implemented.
- ✓ They serve as placeholders for methods that must be implemented by subclasses.
- ✓ Subclasses must provide concrete implementations for these abstract methods.

ENFORCE A CONTRACT:

- ≡ Abstract classes enforce a contract between the abstract class and its subclasses.
- ✓ Subclasses must adhere to the interface defined by the abstract class, implementing all abstract methods to fulfill the contract.

PROMOTE CODE REUSE AND MAINTAINABILITY:

- ≡ Abstract classes promote code reuse by providing a common interface or behavior that can be shared among multiple subclasses.
- ≡ They help in organizing code and promoting maintainability by defining a clear structure for subclasses to follow.
- ✓ Overall, abstract classes in Python provide a powerful mechanism for defining common interfaces and promoting code clarity, reusability, and maintainability.
- ✓ They encourage good design practices by enforcing contracts between classes and facilitating the creation of well-structured object-oriented systems.

Abstract Base Class ← SubClass

- ≡ Subclassing an Abstract Base Class (ABC) in Python involves creating a new class that inherits from the ABC and provides concrete implementations for its abstract methods.

- ≡ This allows you to define a common interface or behavior specified by the ABC and ensure that subclasses adhere to this interface by implementing the required methods.

Steps 1:

Defining An Abc:

First, you define an abstract base class by subclassing ABC from the abc module and using the @abstractmethod decorator to mark methods as abstract.

Steps 2:

Creating Concrete SubClasses:

Then, you create concrete subclasses that inherit from the ABC and provide implementations for its abstract methods.

Steps 3:

Using SubClasses:

Finally, you can instantiate and use the concrete subclasses, which now adhere to the interface defined by the ABC.

Example

```python
from abc import ABC, abstractmethod


class Shape(ABC):
    @abstractmethod
    def area(self):
        pass

    @abstractmethod
    def perimeter(self):
        pass


class Rectangle(Shape):
    def __init__(self, length, width):
        self.length = length
        self.width = width

    def area(self):
        return self.length * self.width

    def perimeter(self):
        return 2 * (self.length + self.width)
```

```python
class Circle(Shape):
    def __init__(self, radius):
        self.radius = radius

    def area(self):
        return 3.14 * self.radius ** 2

    def perimeter(self):
        return 2 * 3.14 * self.radius


# Create instances of concrete subclasses
rectangle = Rectangle(5, 4)
circle = Circle(3)
# Use the concrete subclasses
print("Rectangle Area:", rectangle.area())
print("Rectangle Perimeter:", rectangle.perimeter())
print("Circle Area:", circle.area())
print("Circle Circumference:", circle.perimeter())
```

OUTPUT

```
Rectangle Area: 20
Rectangle Perimeter: 18
```

```
Circle Area: 28.26
Circle Circumference: 18.84
```

EXPLANATION

- Shape is an abstract base class (ABC) that defines two abstract methods: area() and perimeter().
- Rectangle and Circle are concrete subclasses of Shape that provide implementations for the abstract methods.
- Both subclasses adhere to the interface defined by the Shape ABC, ensuring that they provide area() and perimeter() methods.
- You can instantiate and use instances of the concrete subclasses, which now have well-defined behavior specified by the ABC.

CHAPTER 17

OBJECT ORIENTED PROGRAMMING

IN PYTHON

OPERATOR OVERLOADING

INTRODUCTION , CREATE , IMPORT SYNTAX

OPERATOR OVERLOADING ← INTRODUCTION

SPECIAL METHOD (__add__() , __sub__() ,
__mul__() , __str__())

≡ Operator overloading in Python refers to the ability to redefine the behavior of built-in operators ($+$, $-$, $*$, $/$, etc.) for user-defined objects.

≡ By overloading operators, you can customize how objects of a class behave when operated with built-in operators.

≡ Allowing for more natural and intuitive syntax.

✓ To use operator overloading in Python, you need to define special methods, also known as magic methods or dunder methods (due to their double underscore prefix and suffix), that correspond to the operators you want to overload.

✓ These special methods are automatically called when the corresponding operator is used with objects of your class.

EXAMPLE

```python
class Point:
    def __init__(self, x, y):
        self.x = x
        self.y = y

    def __add__(self, other):
        return Point(self.x + other.x, self.y + other.y)

    def __sub__(self, other):
        return Point(self.x - other.x, self.y - other.y)

    def __mul__(self, scalar):
        return Point(self.x * scalar, self.y * scalar)

    def __str__(self):
        return f"({self.x}, {self.y})"

# Create two Point objects
p1 = Point(1, 2)
p2 = Point(3, 4)
# Use the overloaded operators
```

```
print("Addition:", p1 + p2)
print("Subtraction:", p1 - p2)
print("Scalar multiplication:", p1 * 2)
```

OUTPUT

```
Addition: (4, 6)
Subtraction: (-2, -2)
Scalar multiplication: (2, 4)
```

EXPLANATION

- ≡ We define a Point class to represent 2D points with x and y coordinates.
- ≡ We overload the +, -, and * operators by defining special methods __add__, __sub__, and __mul__, respectively.
- ≡ When we use the +, -, and * operators with Point objects, Python automatically calls the corresponding special methods.
- ≡ We also define a __str__ method to customize the string representation of Point objects when using print().

- ✓ Operator overloading allows you to write more expressive and concise code by providing natural syntax for operations on user-defined objects.
- ✓ It's a powerful feature of Python's object-oriented programming model that enables customization of behavior to suit the needs of your classes.

SPECIAL METHOD (__add__())

- ≡ To overload the addition operator (+) for numerical operations in Python, you need to define the special method __add__() within your class.
- ≡ This method will be automatically called when the addition operator is used with instances of your class.

EXAMPLE

```python
class Number:
    def __init__(self, value):
        self.value = value

    def __add__(self, other):

        # Check if 'other' is an instance of Number
        if isinstance(other, Number):

            # If 'other' is an instance of Number, perform addition
            return Number(self.value + other.value)

        else:

            # If 'other' is not an instance of Number, raise
              TypeError
```

```python
        raise TypeError("Unsupported operand type(s) for +:
                '{}' and '{}'".format(
                type(self).__name__, type(other).__name__))

    def __str__(self):
        return str(self.value)

# Create instances of Number
num1 = Number(5)
num2 = Number(10)

# Use the overloaded addition operator
result = num1 + num2
print("Result:", result)
```

OUTPUT

```
Result: 15
```

EXPLANATION

- ≡ We define a Number class that represents a numerical value.
- ≡ We define the __add__() special method, which will be called when the addition operator (+) is used with instances of the Number class.
- ≡ Inside the __add__() method, we check if the other operand is an instance of the Number class. If it is, we perform the

addition of the values and return a new Number object with the result.

- ≡ If the other operand is not an instance of the Number class, we raise a TypeError to indicate that the operation is not supported.
- ≡ We define a __str__() method to provide a string representation of Number objects when they are printed.

- ✓ You can now use the addition operator (+) with instances of the Number class.
- ✓ And Python will automatically call the __add__() method to perform the addition operation.

OPERATOR OVERLOADING ← INTRODUCTION SUBTRACTION(-) SPECIAL METHOD (__sub__())

- ≡ To overload the subtraction operator (-) for numerical operations in Python.
- ≡ You need to define the special method __sub__() within your class.

- ≡ This method will be automatically called when the subtraction operator is used with instances of your class.

EXAMPLE

```
class Number:
   def __init__(self, value):
      self.value = value
```

```python
    def __sub__(self, other):

        # Check if 'other' is an instance of Number
        if isinstance(other, Number):
            # If 'other' is an instance of Number, perform
                subtraction
            return Number(self.value - other.value)

        else:

            # If 'other' is not an instance of Number, raise
                TypeError

            raise TypeError("Unsupported operand type(s) for -:
                    '{}' and '{}'".format(
                    type(self).__name__, type(other).__name__))

    def __str__(self):
        return str(self.value)

# Create instances of Number
num1 = Number(10)
num2 = Number(5)

# Use the overloaded subtraction operator
```

```
result = num1 - num2
print("Result:", result)
```

OUTPUT

```
Result: 5
```

EXPLANATION

- ≡ We define a Number class that represents a numerical value.
- ≡ We define the __sub__() special method, which will be called when the subtraction operator (-) is used with instances of the Number class.

- ≡ Inside the __sub__() method, we check if the other operand is an instance of the Number class.
- ≡ If it is, we perform the subtraction of the values and return a new Number object with the result.

- ≡ If the other operand is not an instance of the Number class.
- ≡ We raise a TypeError to indicate that the operation is not supported.
- ≡ We define a __str__() method to provide a string representation of Number objects when they are printed.

- ✓ You can now use the subtraction operator (-) with instances of the Number class.
- ✓ And Python will automatically call the __sub__() method to perform the subtraction operation.

OPERATOR OVERLOADING←INTRODUCTION MUTIPLICATION(*)

SPECIAL METHOD (__mul__())

- ≡ To overload the multiplication operator (*) for numerical operations in Python.
- ≡ You need to define the special method __mul__() within your class.
- ≡ This method will be automatically called when the multiplication operator is used with instances of your class.

EXAMPLE

```python
class Number:
    def __init__(self, value):
        self.value = value

    def __mul__(self, other):

        # Check if 'other' is an instance of Number
        if isinstance(other, Number):

            # If 'other' is an instance of Number, perform
                multiplication
            return Number(self.value * other.value)

        else:

            # If 'other' is not an instance of Number, raise
```

```
        TypeError
            raise TypeError("Unsupported operand type(s) for *:
                    '{}' and '{}'".format(
                type(self).__name__, type(other).__name__))


    def __str__(self):
        return str(self.value)

# Create instances of Number
num1 = Number(5)
num2 = Number(10)

# Use the overloaded multiplication operator
result = num1 * num2
print("Result:", result)
```

OUTPUT

```
Result: 50
```

EXPLANATION

- ≡ We define a Number class that represents a numerical value.
- ≡ We define the __mul__() special method, which will be called when the multiplication operator (*) is used with instances of the Number class.

- ≡ Inside the __mul__() method, we check if the other operand is an instance of the Number class.
- ≡ If it is, we perform the multiplication of the values and return a new Number object with the result.

- ≡ If the other operand is not an instance of the Number class, we raise a TypeError to indicate that the operation is not supported.
- ≡ We define a __str__() method to provide a string representation of Number objects when they are printed.

- ✓ You can now use the multiplication operator (*) with instances of the Number class.
- ✓ And Python will automatically call the __mul__() method to perform the multiplication operation.

OPERATOR OVERLOADING ← INTRODUCTION LESS THAN (<) SPECIAL METHOD (__lt__())

- ≡ To overload the less than operator (<) for comparison operations in Python.
- ≡ You need to define the special method __lt__() within your class.

- ≡ This method will be automatically called when the less than operator is used with instances of your class.

EXAMPLE

```
class Number:
```

```python
    def __init__(self, value):
        self.value = value

    def __lt__(self, other):

        # Check if 'other' is an instance of Number
        if isinstance(other, Number):

            # If 'other' is an instance of Number, perform
              comparison
            return self.value < other.value

        else:

            # If 'other' is not an instance of Number, raise
              TypeError
            raise TypeError("Unsupported operand type(s) for <:
                    '{}' and '{}'".format(
                type(self).__name__, type(other).__name__))

# Create instances of Number
num1 = Number(5)
num2 = Number(10)
```

```
# Use the overloaded less than operator
result = num1 < num2
print("Result:", result)
```

OUTPUT

```
Result: True
```

EXPLANATION

- ≡ We define a Number class that represents a numerical value.
- ≡ We define the __lt__() special method, which will be called when the less than operator (<) is used with instances of the Number class.

- ≡ Inside the __lt__() method, we check if the other operand is an instance of the Number class.
- ≡ If it is, we compare the values and return True if the value of the current object is less than the value of the other object, otherwise False.

- ≡ If the other operand is not an instance of the Number class.
- ≡ We raise a TypeError to indicate that the operation is not supported.

- ✓ You can now use the less than operator (<) with instances of the Number class.
- ✓ And Python will automatically call the __lt__() method to perform the comparison operation.

SPECIAL METHOD (__eq__())

- ≡ To overload the equal to operator (==) for comparison operations in Python.
- ≡ You need to define the special method __eq__() within your class.

- ≡ This method will be automatically called when the equal to operator is used with instances of your class.

EXAMPLE

```
class Number:
  def __init__(self, value):
    self.value = value

  def __eq__(self, other):

    # Check if 'other' is an instance of Number
    if isinstance(other, Number):

      # If 'other' is an instance of Number, perform
        comparison
      return self.value == other.value

    else:
```

```
            # If 'other' is not an instance of Number, return False
            return False

# Create instances of Number
num1 = Number(5)
num2 = Number(5)
num3 = Number(10)

# Use the overloaded equal to operator
result1 = num1 == num2
result2 = num1 == num3
print("Result1:", result1)
print("Result2:", result2)
```

OUTPUT

```
Result1: True
Result2: False
```

EXPLANATION

- ≡ We define a Number class that represents a numerical value.
- ≡ We define the __eq__() special method, which will be called when the equal to operator (==) is used with instances of the Number class.

≡ Inside the __eq__() method, we check if the other operand is an instance of the Number class.

≡ If it is, we compare the values and return True if the value of the current object is equal to the value of the other object, otherwise False.

≡ If the other operand is not an instance of the Number class, we return False.

✓ You can now use the equal to operator (==) with instances of the Number class

✓ And Python will automatically call the __eq__() method to perform the comparison operation.

OPERATOR OVERLOADING ← INTRODUCTION NOT EQUAL(!=) SPECIAL METHOD (__ne__())

≡ To overload the not equal to operator (!=) for comparison operations in Python.

≡ You need to define the special method __ne__() within your class.

≡ This method will be automatically called when the not equal to operator is used with instances of your class.

EXAMPLE

```python
class Number:
    def __init__(self, value):
        self.value = value
```

```python
    def __ne__(self, other):

        # Check if 'other' is an instance of Number
        if isinstance(other, Number):

            # If 'other' is an instance of Number, perform
                comparison
            return self.value != other.value

        else:

            # If 'other' is not an instance of Number, return True
            return True

# Create instances of Number
num1 = Number(5)
num2 = Number(5)
num3 = Number(10)

# Use the overloaded not equal to operator
result1 = num1 != num2
result2 = num1 != num3
print("Result1:", result1)
print("Result2:", result2)
```

OUTPUT

Result1: False

Result2: True

EXPLANATION

- ≡ We define a Number class that represents a numerical value.
- ≡ We define the __ne__() special method, which will be called when the not equal to operator (!=) is used with instances of the Number class.

- ≡ Inside the __ne__() method, we check if the other operand is an instance of the Number class.
- ≡ If it is, we compare the values and return True if the value of the current object is not equal to the value of the other object, otherwise False.

- ≡ If the other operand is not an instance of the Number class, we return True.

- ✓ You can now use the not equal to operator (!=) with instances of the Number class.
- ✓ And Python will automatically call the __ne__() method to perform the comparison operation.

Operator Overloading ← Introduction Greater Than(>) Special Method (__gt__())

- ≡ To overload the greater than operator (>) for comparison operations in Python.
- ≡ You need to define the special method __gt__() within your class.
- ≡ This method will be automatically called when the greater than operator is used with instances of your class.

Example

```python
class Number:
    def __init__(self, value):
        self.value = value

    def __gt__(self, other):

        # Check if 'other' is an instance of Number
        if isinstance(other, Number):

            # If 'other' is an instance of Number, perform
            comparison
            return self.value > other.value

        else:
```

```
              # If 'other' is not an instance of Number, raise
                TypeError
              raise TypeError("Unsupported operand type(s) for >:
                          '{}' and '{}'".format(
                    type(self).__name__, type(other).__name__))


# Create instances of Number
num1 = Number(10)
num2 = Number(5)

# Use the overloaded greater than operator
result = num1 > num2
print("Result:", result)
```

OUTPUT

```
Result: True
```

EXPLANATION

≡ We define a Number class that represents a numerical
  value.
≡ We define the __gt__() special method, which will be
  called when the greater than operator (>) is used with
  instances of the Number class.

≡ Inside the __gt__() method, we check if the other operand
  is an instance of the Number class.

- ≡ If it is, we compare the values and return True if the value of the current object is greater than the value of the other object, otherwise False.

- ≡ If the other operand is not an instance of the Number class, we raise a TypeError to indicate that the operation is not supported.

- ✓ You can now use the greater than operator (>) with instances of the Number class
- ✓ And Python will automatically call the __gt__() method to perform the comparison operation.

OPERATOR OVERLOADING ← INTRODUCTION AND (and)

SPECIAL METHOD (__and__())

- ≡ To overload the logical and operator (and) for boolean operations in Python.
- ≡ You need to define the special method __and__() within your class.

- ≡ This method will be automatically called when the logical and operator is used with instances of your class.

EXAMPLE

```python
class MyClass:
    def __init__(self, value):
        self.value = value
```

```python
def __and__(self, other):

    # Check if 'other' is an instance of MyClass
    if isinstance(other, MyClass):

        # If 'other' is an instance of MyClass, perform logical
            and
        return self.value and other.value

    else:

        # If 'other' is not an instance of MyClass, raise
            TypeError
        raise TypeError("Unsupported operand type(s) for
                        logical and: '{}' and '{}'".format(
            type(self).__name__, type(other).__name__))

# Create instances of MyClass
obj1 = MyClass(True)
obj2 = MyClass(False)
```

```
# Use the overloaded logical and operator
result = obj1 and obj2
print("Result:", result)
```

OUTPUT

```
Result: False
```

EXPLANATION

- ≡ We define a MyClass class that represents an object with a boolean value.
- ≡ We define the __and__() special method, which will be called when the logical and operator (and) is used with instances of the MyClass class.

- ≡ Inside the __and__() method, we check if the other operand is an instance of the MyClass class.
- ≡ If it is, we perform the logical and operation of the boolean values and return the result.

- ≡ If the other operand is not an instance of the MyClass class, we raise a TypeError to indicate that the operation is not supported.

- ✓ You can now use the logical and operator (and) with instances of the MyClass class.
- ✓ And Python will automatically call the __and__() method to perform the boolean operation.

CHAPTER 18

FILE IN PYTHON

INTRODUCTION , ACCESS MODE , HANDLER , APPEND , CREATE …

FILE ← INTRODUCTION

- ≡ In Python , file is which contains your Python code. Where you are writing your code to run with extension . py .

FILE : ACCESS MODE

FILE ← ACCESS MODE

- ≡ Python file access modes are used to specify the mode in which a file is opened.
- ≡ Each mode determines the operations that can be performed on the file.
- ≡ Reading, writing, appending, or creating a new file.
- ≡ Here are the commonly used file access modes in Python.

('r') OPEN A FILE IN READ MODE:

- ≡ If the file does not exist or cannot be opened, an IOError will be raised.

```
# Open a file in read mode

with open('file.txt', 'r') as file:
    content = file.read()
    print(content)
```

('w') OPEN A FILE IN WRITE MODE:

≡ If the file already exists, its contents will be overwritten. If the file does not exist, it will be created.

EXAMPLE

```
# Open a file in write mode

with open('file.txt', 'w') as file:
    file.write('Hello, world!')
```

('a') OPEN A FILE IN APPEND MODE:

≡ The file pointer is positioned at the end of the file.
≡ New data will be written to the end of the file. If the file does not exist, it will be created.

EXAMPLE

```
# Open a file in append mode
```

```
with open('file.txt', 'a') as file:

    file.write('\nAppending new content')
```

('r+') OPEN A FILE IN READ AND WRITE MODE:

- ≡ The file pointer is positioned at the beginning of the file.
- ≡ If the file does not exist or cannot be opened, an IOError will be raised.

EXAMPLE

```
# Open a file in read and write mode


with open('file.txt', 'r+') as file:

    content = file.read()

    file.write('\nAdding new content')
```

('w+') OPEN A FILE IN READ AND WRITE MODE:

- ≡ If the file already exists, its contents will be overwritten.
- ≡ If the file does not exist, it will be created.

EXAMPLE

```
# Open a file in read and write mode

 (creating a new file if it doesn't exist)
```

```
with open('new_file.txt', 'w+') as file:
    file.write('This is a new file')
```

('a+') Open a File In Read And Append Mode:

- ≡ The file pointer is positioned at the end of the file.
- ≡ New data will be written to the end of the file.
- ≡ If the file does not exist, it will be created.

Example

```
# Open a file in read and append mode
 (creating a new file if it doesn't exist)

with open('new_file.txt', 'a+') as file:
    file.write('\nThis is appended content')
```

- ✓ Remember to always close the file using the with statement or by explicitly calling the close() method after you are done working with it.
- ✓ This ensures that any resources used by the file are properly released.

FILE :

FILE ← HANDLER

- ≡ In Python, a file handler (also referred to as a file object or file descriptor) is an object that represents an open file.
- ≡ It provides methods and attributes that allow you to interact with the file.
- ≡ Such as reading from it, writing to it, or manipulating its contents.

- ✓ File handlers are typically obtained by calling the open() function.
- ✓ Which returns a file handler associated with the specified file.
- ✓ You can then use this file handler to perform various operations on the file.

EXAMPLE

```python
# Open a file in read mode and obtain a file handler
file_handler = open('file.txt', 'r')

# Read the entire contents of the file
content = file_handler.read()
print(content)

# Close the file handler when done
file_handler.close()
```

EXPLANATION

- ≡ We use the open() function to open a file named 'file.txt' in read mode ('r').
- ≡ This returns a file handler that represents the opened file.

- ≡ We then use the read() method of the file handler.
- ≡ To read the entire contents of the file and store it in the variable content.

- ≡ Finally, we close the file handler by calling its close() method.
- ≡ It's important to close file handlers when they are no longer needed to free up system resources and ensure that any buffered data is flushed to the file.

CONTEXT MANAGER (WITH STATEMENT):

- ≡ Python supports a context manager (with statement) for file handling.
- ≡ Which automatically closes the file handler when you exit the block.
- ≡ This is the recommended way to work with files in Python.

EXAMPLE

```
# Open a file using a context manager

with open('file.txt', 'r') as file_handler:
    content = file_handler.read()
```

```
print(content)
```

EXPLANATION

In this example, the file handler is automatically closed when the code block exits, regardless of whether an exception occurs.

Using a context manager helps ensure that file resources are properly managed and avoids the need for explicit calls to close().

FILE ← APPEND

- ≡ To append data to a file using a file handler in Python.
- ≡ You can open the file in append mode ('a').
- ≡ And then use the file handler's write() method to add the desired content to the end of the file.

EXAMPLE

```
# Open the file in append mode and obtain a file handler
with open('file.txt', 'a') as file_handler:

    # Write data to the file
    file_handler.write('\nNew data to be appended')
```

EXPLANATION

- ≡ We open the file 'file.txt' in append mode ('a') using a context manager (with statement).
- ≡ Which automatically closes the file handler when done.

- Inside the context manager block, we use the file handler's write() method.
- To append the string 'New data to be appended' to the file.
- The \n character is used to add a new line before the appended data.

- ✓ After executing this code, the file 'file.txt' will contain the original contents, followed by the new data appended at the end.
- ✓ It's worth noting that the file will be created if it does not already exist.
- ✓ If you want to append data to an existing file, ensure it's present in the specified location.

FILE ← CREATE

- To create and write content to a file using a file handler in Python.
- You can open the file in write mode ('w').
- And then use the file handler's write() method to add the desired content.

EXAMPLE

```
# Open the file in write mode and obtain a file handler
with open('file.txt', 'w') as file_handler:

    # Write data to the file
```

```
file_handler.write('This is some content that we are writing
to the file.\n')


file_handler.write('This is another line of content.\n')
```

EXPLANATION

- ≡ We open the file 'file.txt' in write mode ('w') using a context manager (with statement), which automatically closes the file handler when done.
- ≡ Inside the context manager block, we use the file handler's write() method to write the desired content to the file. Each call to write() adds the specified string to the file.

- ✓ After executing this code, the file 'file.txt' will contain the content that we wrote to it.
- ✓ If the file already exists, its contents will be overwritten.
- ✓ If you want to append content to an existing file or preserve its current contents, you should use append mode ('a') instead of write mode ('w').

FILE ← READING POSITION

- ≡ In Python, you can use the tell() method of a file object to get the current position of the file cursor (also known as the file pointer).
- ≡ The file cursor represents the position within the file where the next read or write operation will occur.

EXAMPLE

```
# Open the file in read mode and obtain a file handler
with open('file.txt', 'r') as file_handler:

    # Get the current position of the file cursor
    position = file_handler.tell()
    print("Current position:", position)
```

EXPLANATION

- ≡ We use the open() function with the file name 'file.txt' and the mode 'r' to open the file in read mode.
- ≡ We use a context manager (with statement) to automatically close the file handler after it's been opened.
- ≡ Inside the context manager block, we call the tell() method of the file handler to get the current position of the file cursor.
- ≡ We print the current position of the file cursor to the console.

- ✓ The value returned by tell() is an integer representing the byte offset from the beginning of the file.
- ✓ The first byte in the file is at position 0, the second byte is at position 1, and so on.

FILE ← SEEKING POSITION

- ≡ In Python, you can use the seek() method of a file object to change the position of the file cursor (file pointer) within the file.
- ≡ The seek() method takes two arguments: the offset and the optional whence parameter.

EXAMPLE

```
# Open the file in read mode and obtain a file handler
with open('file.txt', 'r') as file_handler:

    # Set the file cursor to a specific position
       (e.g., byte 10 from the beginning of the file)
    file_handler.seek(10)

    # Read data from the new cursor position
    data = file_handler.read()
    print("Data from position 10:", data)

    # Move the cursor 5 bytes forward from the current position
    file_handler.seek(5, 1)

    # Read data from the new cursor position
    data = file_handler.read()
```

```
print("Data from current position + 5:", data)


# Move the cursor to the end of the file
file_handler.seek(0, 2)


# Read data from the end of the file
data = file_handler.read()
print("Data from the end of the file:", data)
```

EXPLANATION

≡ We use the open() function with the file name 'file.txt' and the mode 'r' to open the file in read mode.
≡ We use a context manager (with statement) to automatically close the file handler after it's been opened.
≡ We use the seek() method to change the position of the file cursor:
- ✓ seek(10) sets the cursor to byte 10 from the beginning of the file.
- ✓ seek(5, 1) moves the cursor 5 bytes forward from the current position.
- ✓ seek(0, 2) sets the cursor to the end of the file.
≡ We then read data from the file at the new cursor positions using the read() method.
✓ By using seek(), you can navigate within the file to read or modify specific portions of its content.

FILE ← SIZE

You can use the os.path.getsize() function from the os module to get the size of a file in bytes.

EXAMPLE

```
import os


# Get the size of the file

file_size = os.path.getsize('file.txt')


print("File size:", file_size, "bytes")
```

EXPLANATION

- ≡ We import the os module.
- ≡ We use the os.path.getsize() function, passing the path to the file ('file.txt' in this case) as an argument.
- ≡ The function returns the size of the file in bytes, which we store in the variable file_size.
- ≡ We print the size of the file to the console.

- ✓ This method allows you to quickly retrieve the size of a file without needing to open it or read its contents.

FILE ← DELETE

- ≡ To delete a file in Python, you can use the os.remove() function from the os module.

EXAMPLE

```python
import os

# File path
file_path = 'file_to_delete.txt'

# Check if the file exists before attempting to delete it
if os.path.exists(file_path):

    # Delete the file
    os.remove(file_path)
    print("File deleted successfully!")
else:
    print("File does not exist.")
```

EXPLANATION

- ≡ We import the os module.
- ≡ We define the path of the file we want to delete.
- ≡ We use the os.path.exists() function to check if the file exists before attempting to delete it.
- ≡ If the file exists, we use the os.remove() function, passing the file path as an argument, to delete the file.
- ≡ If the file does not exist, we print a message indicating that the file does not exist.
- ✓ Make sure to replace 'file_to_delete.txt' with the actual path of the file you want to delete.

FILE : INTRODUCTION

(r) READ VS (r+) READ , WRITE VS (w+) WRITE , READ MODE
← INTRODUCTION

(r) READ MODE: ← INTRODUCTION

- ≡ This mode opens the file for reading only.
- ≡ If the file does not exist or cannot be opened, it will raise an IOError exception.
- ≡ The file pointer is positioned at the beginning of the file.
- ≡ You cannot write to the file in this mode.

(r+) READ , WRITE MODE: ← INTRODUCTION

- ≡ This mode opens the file for both reading and writing.
- ≡ If the file does not exist or cannot be opened, it will raise an IOError exception.
- ≡ The file pointer is positioned at the beginning of the file.
- ≡ You can read from and write to the file in this mode.

(w+) WRITE , READ MODE: ← INTRODUCTION

- ≡ This mode opens the file for both reading and writing.
- ≡ If the file does not exist, it will be created.
- ≡ If the file exists, its contents will be overwritten.
- ≡ The file pointer is positioned at the beginning of the file.

(r) READ MODE:

EXAMPLE

```python
# Open the file in read mode
with open('file.txt', 'r') as file_handler:

    # Read data from the file
    content = file_handler.read()
    print("Content from 'r' mode:", content)

    # Try to write data to the file (will raise an IOError)
    try:
        file_handler.write("Trying to write in 'r' mode.")
    except IOError as e:
        print("Error:", e)
```

(r+) READ , WRITE MODE:

EXAMPLE

```python
# Open the file in read and write mode
with open('file.txt', 'r+') as file_handler:

    # Read data from the file
    content = file_handler.read()
```

```
print("Content from 'r+' mode:", content)


# Move the file cursor to the beginning
file_handler.seek(0)


# Write data to the file
file_handler.write("Writing in 'r+' mode.")


# Move the file cursor to the end
file_handler.seek(0, 2)


# Read data from the file
content = file_handler.read()
print("New content from 'r+' mode:", content)
```

(w+) WRITE , READ MODE:

EXAMPLE

```
# Open the file in write and read mode
with open('file.txt', 'w+') as file_handler:
    # Write data to the file
    file_handler.write("Writing data in 'w+' mode.")
```

```
# Move the file cursor to the beginning
file_handler.seek(0)

# Read data from the file
content = file_handler.read()
print("Content from 'w+' mode:", content)
```

EXPLANATION

- ✓ In the example with 'r' mode, we attempt to write data to the file after reading from it, which results in an IOError because the file was opened in read-only mode.

- ✓ In the example with 'r+' mode, we can both read from and write to the file, as demonstrated by reading the file contents, writing new content to it, and then reading the updated contents.

- ✓ In the example with 'w+' mode, we write new content to the file, and then read the contents back.
- ✓ If the file already existed, its contents would be overwritten by the new content we write.
- ✓ If the file didn't exist, it would be created.

CHAPTER 19

TEXT FILE IN PYTHON

INTRODUCTION , READ , PATH , LINE , WRITE ...

TEXT FILE ← READ

- ≡ To read from a file in Python, you can use the open() function to open the file.
- ≡ And obtain a file handler, and then use methods like read(), readline(), or readlines() to read the content from the file.

READING THE ENTIRE CONTENTS OF A FILE AT ONCE USING read():

EXAMPLE

```python
# Open the file in read mode and obtain a file handler
with open('file.txt', 'r') as file_handler:

    # Read the entire contents of the file
    content = file_handler.read()
    print(content)
```

READING ONE LINE AT A TIME USING readline():
EXAMPLE

```python
# Open the file in read mode and obtain a file handler
with open('file.txt', 'r') as file_handler:


    # Read one line at a time
    line = file_handler.readline()
    while line:


        # end='' to avoid adding extra newlines
        print(line, end='')
        line = file_handler.readline()
```

READING ALL LINES INTO A LIST USING readlines():
EXAMPLE

```python
# Open the file in read mode and obtain a file handler
with open('file.txt', 'r') as file_handler:
    # Read all lines into a list
    lines = file_handler.readlines()
    for line in lines:
        # end='' to avoid adding extra newlines
        print(line, end='')
```

EXPLANATION

- ≡ We use the open() function with the file name 'file.txt' and the mode 'r' to open the file in read mode.
- ≡ We use a context manager (with statement) to automatically close the file handler after it's been opened.
- ≡ We use one of the file handler's methods (read(), readline(), or readlines()) to read the content from the file.
- ≡ We print the content to the console.

- ✓ Choose the appropriate method based on your specific requirements.
- ✓ If you want to process the entire content of the file at once, use read().
- ✓ If you want to process the file line by line, use readline().
- ✓ If you want to store all lines in a list, use readlines().

TEXT FILE ← PATH

- ≡ In Python, you can obtain both relative and absolute file paths using various methods.

USING THE os.path MODULE:

- ≡ The os.path.abspath() function returns the absolute path of a file.
- ≡ The os.path.relpath() function returns the relative path of a file from a specified directory (or the current working directory if not specified).

EXAMPLE

```
import os

# Absolute path
absolute_path = os.path.abspath('file.txt')
print("Absolute path:", absolute_path)

# Relative path from the current working directory
relative_path = os.path.relpath('file.txt')
print("Relative path:", relative_path)
```

USING THE pathlib MODULE:

- ≡ The pathlib.Path.resolve() method returns the absolute path of a file.

≡ The pathlib.Path.relative_to() method returns the relative path of a file from a specified directory.

EXAMPLE

```
from pathlib import Path

# Absolute path
absolute_path = Path('file.txt').resolve()
print("Absolute path:", absolute_path)

# Relative path from the current working directory
relative_path = Path('file.txt').relative_to(Path.cwd())
print("Relative path:", relative_path)
```

USING THE os.getcwd() FUNCTION
(TO GET THE CURRENT WORKING DIRECTORY):

≡ The os.getcwd() function returns the current working directory.

≡ You can combine this with relative file paths to get the absolute paths.

EXAMPLE

```
import os
```

```
# Current working directory
cwd = os.getcwd()

# Relative file path
relative_path = 'file.txt'

# Absolute path
absolute_path = os.path.join(cwd, relative_path)
print("Absolute path:", absolute_path)
```

Choose the method that best fits your requirements and coding style.

The pathlib module is recommended for its object-oriented interface and improved readability.

TEXT FILE ← WRITE

≡ To write a line to a file using Python, you can use the write() method of the file object.

EXAMPLE

```python
# Open the file in write mode and obtain a file handler
with open('output.txt', 'w') as file_handler:

    # Write a line to the file
    file_handler.write("This is a line written to the file.\n")
```

EXPLANATION

≡ We use the open() function with the file name 'output.txt' and the mode 'w' to open the file in write mode.

≡ If the file does not exist, it will be created. If the file already exists, its contents will be overwritten.

≡ We use a context manager (with statement) to automatically close the file handler after it's been opened.

≡ We use the write() method of the file handler to write the specified line to the file.

≡ The '\n' character is used to add a newline at the end of the line.

✓ After executing this code, the file 'output.txt' will contain the line "This is a line written to the file." followed by a newline character.

CHAPTER 20

EXCEPTION IN PYTHON

INTRODUCTION , TRY - EXCEPT ,

ELSE , CATCH , FINALLY , WRITE ...

EXCEPTION ← INTRODUCTION

- ≡ An exception in Python is an event that occurs during the execution of a program.
- ≡ That disrupts the normal flow of the program's instructions.

- ≡ When an exceptional condition arises, such as an error or unexpected behavior, **Python** raises an exception to handle the situation.
- ≡ Exceptions allow you to handle errors in a controlled manner, such as by displaying an error message, logging the error, or taking corrective action.

EXCEPTION ← USE

HANDLE ERRORS:

- ≡ Exceptions allow you to detect and handle errors that occur during the execution of your program.
- ≡ This helps prevent program crashes and provides a way to gracefully recover from errors.

PROVIDE FEEDBACK TO USERS:

- ≡ Exceptions allow you to provide informative error messages to users, helping them understand what went wrong and how to resolve the issue.

LOG ERRORS:

- ≡ Exceptions can be logged to record information about errors that occur during program execution.
- ≡ This can be useful for debugging and troubleshooting.

TAKE CORRECTIVE ACTION:

- ≡ Exceptions can be caught and handled by executing specific code to address the error condition, such as retrying an operation, using default values, or prompting the user for input.

SYNTAX

```
try:
    # Attempting division by zero
```

```
    result = 10 / 0

except ZeroDivisionError:
    print("Error: Division by zero")
```

EXPLANATION

- ≡ The code inside the try block attempts to divide 10 by zero, which would result in a ZeroDivisionError.
- ≡ The except block catches the ZeroDivisionError exception and prints an error message indicating that division by zero occurred.
- ≡ By handling the exception, the program continues to execute normally without crashing.

EXCEPTION ← TRY - EXCEPT

≡ In Python, you use the try and except blocks to handle exceptions.

SYNTAX

```
try:
    # Code that may raise an exception
    # ...
except ExceptionType:
    # Code to handle the exception
    # ...
```

EXPLANATION

≡ The try block contains the code that may raise an exception.
≡ It's the block where you expect the potential error to occur.

≡ The except block specifies the type of exception that you want to catch and handle.
≡ If an exception of the specified type (or a subclass of it) occurs within the try block, the corresponding except block is executed.

EXAMPLE

```
try:
    # Code that may raise an exception
```

```python
num1 = int(input("Enter a number: "))
num2 = int(input("Enter another number: "))
result = num1 / num2
print("Result:", result)


except ValueError:
    # Handle ValueError (e.g., invalid input)
    print("Please enter valid integers.")


except ZeroDivisionError:
    # Handle ZeroDivisionError (e.g., division by zero)
    print("Error: Division by zero is not allowed.")


except Exception as e:
    # Handle any other type of exception
    print("An error occurred:", e)
```

EXPLANATION

- ≡ The try block attempts to perform division operation between two numbers entered by the user.
- ≡ If a ValueError occurs (e.g., if the user inputs non-integer values), the corresponding except ValueError block handles it.

≡ If a ZeroDivisionError occurs (e.g., if the user inputs 0 as the second number), the corresponding except ZeroDivisionError block handles it.

≡ If any other type of exception occurs, it will be caught by the except Exception block, and the error message will be printed.

≡ If no exception occurs within the try block, the except block(s) will be skipped, and the program will continue execution after the try-except statement.

EXCEPTION ← ELSE

≡ In Python, you can use a try...else block to handle exceptions in a way that distinguishes between the code that may raise an exception and the code that should run if no exception occurs.

≡ The else block is executed only if no exception is raised in the try block.

SYNTAX

```
try:
    # Code that may raise an exception
    # ...
except ExceptionType:
    # Code to handle the exception
    # ...
```

```
else:
    # Code to execute if no exception occurs
    # ...
```

EXPLANATION

- The try block contains the code that may raise an exception.
- This is the block where you expect the potential error to occur.

- The except block specifies the type of exception that you want to catch and handle.
- If an exception of the specified type (or a subclass of it) occurs within the try block, the corresponding except block is executed.

- The else block contains code that should run if no exception occurs in the try block.
- It is optional and is executed only if no exception is raised.

EXAMPLE

```
try:
    # Code that may raise an exception
    num1 = int(input("Enter a number: "))
    num2 = int(input("Enter another number: "))
    result = num1 / num2
```

```python
except ValueError:
    # Handle ValueError (e.g., invalid input)
    print("Please enter valid integers.")

except ZeroDivisionError:
    # Handle ZeroDivisionError (e.g., division by zero)
    print("Error: Division by zero is not allowed.")

else:
    # Code to execute if no exception occurs
    print("Result:", result)
```

EXPLANATION

- ≡ The try block attempts to perform a division operation between two numbers entered by the user.
- ≡ If a ValueError occurs (e.g., if the user inputs non-integer values), the corresponding except ValueError block handles it.

- ≡ If a ZeroDivisionError occurs (e.g., if the user inputs 0 as the second number), the corresponding except ZeroDivisionError block handles it.
- ≡ If no exception occurs within the try block, the else block is executed, and the result is printed.

EXCEPTION ← FINALLY

≡ In Python, the finally clause is used in conjunction with the try statement to define a block of code that is always executed, regardless of whether an exception occurs or not.

≡ The finally block is commonly used to perform cleanup actions, such as closing files or releasing resources, ensuring that these actions are executed even if an exception is raised.

SYNTAX

```
try:
    # Code that may raise an exception
    # ...
except ExceptionType:
    # Code to handle the exception
    # ...
finally:
    # Code that is always executed
    # ...
```

EXPLANATION

≡ The try block contains the code that may raise an exception.

≡ This is the block where you expect the potential error to occur.

- The except block specifies the type of exception that you want to catch and handle.
- If an exception of the specified type (or a subclass of it) occurs within the try block, the corresponding except block is executed.

- The finally block contains code that is always executed, regardless of whether an exception occurs in the try block or not.

EXAMPLE

```python
try:
    # Open a file
    file_handler = open('file.txt', 'r')

    # Read data from the file
    data = file_handler.read()
    print("Data from file:", data)

except FileNotFoundError:
    print("File not found.")

finally:
    # Close the file (cleanup action)
```

```
file_handler.close()
print("File closed.")
```

EXPLANATION

≡ The try block attempts to open a file 'file.txt' for reading and read its contents.

≡ If a FileNotFoundError occurs (e.g., if the file does not exist), the corresponding except FileNotFoundError block handles it.

≡ The finally block ensures that the file is closed using the close() method, even if an exception occurs or not.

≡ This cleanup action is executed regardless of whether an exception is raised, ensuring that the file is properly closed and resources are released.

EXCEPTION ← CUSTOM

≡ To define a custom exception in Python, you can create a new class that inherits from the built-in Exception class or one of its subclasses.

SYNTAX

```
class CustomError(Exception):
    """Custom exception class."""
    def __init__(self, message="An error occurred"):
        self.message = message
        super().__init__(self.message)
```

EXPLANATION

≡ We define a new class CustomError that inherits from the built-in Exception class.

≡ This makes CustomError a custom exception class.

≡ Inside the class definition, we define an __init__ method to initialize the exception object.

≡ We provide an optional message parameter with a default value of "An error occurred".

≡ This allows us to customize the error message when creating an instance of the CustomError class.

≡ In the __init__ method, we assign the value of the message parameter to the self.message attribute of the exception object.

≡ We call the super().__init__(self.message) method to initialize the base class (Exception) with the custom error message.

Once the custom exception class is defined, you can raise instances of it in your code just like any other exception.

EXAMPLE

```
try:
    # Raise a custom exception
    raise CustomError("This is a custom error message")


except CustomError as e:
    # Handle the custom exception
    print("Custom error:", e.message)
```

EXPLANATION

≡ In this example, when the raise CustomError("This is a custom error message") statement is executed, a CustomError exception is raised with the specified error message.

≡ The except CustomError as e: block catches the custom exception, and the error message (e.message) is printed to

CHAPTER 21

TESTING IN PYTHON

INTRODUCTION , PYTEST INSTALL , PYTEST TEST CASES

TESTING ← INTRODUCTION

- ≡ Unit testing is a software testing technique where individual units or components of a software application are tested in isolation to ensure they behave as expected.
- ≡ In Python, unit testing is commonly performed using the built-in unittest module or third-party libraries like pytest.

WHEN TO USEIT:

- ≡ Unit testing is typically performed during the development phase of a software project.
- ≡ It is used to validate the behavior of individual units or functions in the codebase.

- ≡ Unit tests help ensure that each unit of code works correctly in isolation before integrating them into the larger system.
- ≡ Unit testing is an essential part of the Test-Driven Development (TDD) process, where tests are written before the actual code implementation.

WHY IT'S NEEDED:

IDENTIFY BUGS EARLY:

≡ Unit tests can catch bugs early in the development process, making them easier and cheaper to fix.

ENSURE CODE QUALITY:

≡ Unit tests help maintain code quality by providing a safety net for refactoring and code changes.

≡ They ensure that existing functionality remains intact as the codebase evolves.

FACILITATE COLLABORATION:

≡ Unit tests serve as documentation for how a piece of code should behave.

≡ They make it easier for developers to understand and collaborate on the codebase.

PROMOTE CONFIDENCE:

≡ Having a comprehensive suite of unit tests gives developers confidence that their code works as intended.

≡ It allows them to make changes with the assurance that existing functionality won't be inadvertently broken.

HOW TO WRITE UNIT TESTS:

≡ In Python, unit tests are written using the unittest framework or other testing libraries like pytest.

- ≡ You define test cases as subclasses of unittest.TestCase and write test methods that verify the behavior of individual functions or classes.
- ≡ Test methods typically use assertions to check expected outcomes against actual results.

EXAMPLE

```python
import unittest

def add(x, y):
    return x + y

class TestAddFunction(unittest.TestCase):
    def test_add_positive_numbers(self):
        self.assertEqual(add(2, 3), 5)

    def test_add_negative_numbers(self):
        self.assertEqual(add(-2, -3), -5)

if __name__ == '__main__':
    unittest.main()
```

EXPLANATION

- ≡ In this example, we define a simple add function and write unit tests to verify its behavior for different input scenarios.

TESTING ← PYTEST INSTALL

- ≡ You can install pytest using pip, the package installer for Python.

SYNTAX

```
pip install pytest
```

EXPLANATION

- ≡ You can run this command in your terminal or command prompt to install pytest.
- ≡ Make sure you have pip installed and configured properly in your Python environment.

- ✓ Once pytest is installed, you can use it to write and run tests for your Python code.

TESTING ← PYTEST TEST CASES

- ≡ To create test cases using pytest in Python, you typically organize your test code in separate Python files and use functions prefixed with test_ to define individual test cases.
- ≡ Here's a step-by-step guide on how to create test cases using pytest.

STEP 1:

INSTALL PYTEST:

If you haven't already installed pytest, you can do so using pip .

```
pip install pytest
```

STEP 2:

CREATE A PYTHON FILE FOR YOUR TEST CODE:

- ≡ Create a new Python file (e.g., test_example.py) where you'll write your test cases.
- ≡ This file should contain functions that define your test cases.

STEP 3:

WRITE TEST FUNCTIONS:

- ≡ Write test functions using the test_ prefix to indicate that they are test cases.
- ≡ Within these functions, use assertions to verify the expected behavior of the code being tested.

EXAMPLE

```
# test_example.py

def add(x, y):
    return x + y


def test_add_positive_numbers():
    assert add(2, 3) == 5


def test_add_negative_numbers():
    assert add(-2, -3) == -5
```

- ≡ In this example, we have two test functions
  (test_add_positive_numbers and
  test_add_negative_numbers) that test the add function for
  different scenarios.

STEP 4:

RUN PYTEST:

- ≡ To run your tests, navigate to the directory containing your
  test file(s) in your terminal or command prompt, and run
  the pytest command.

```
Pytest
```

- ≡ pytest will automatically discover and run any test functions defined in files with names that start with test_.
- ≡ It will display the results of the tests, including any failures or errors.
- ≡ You can also specify the name of the test file(s) or directories containing test files to run specific tests.

```
pytest test_example.py
```

This command runs only the tests defined in test_example.py.